War
∽ Ain't No ∾
Picnic

30 CIVIL WAR STORIES & DEVOTIONALS

War
✺ Ain't No ✺
Picnic

30 CIVIL WAR STORIES & DEVOTIONALS

TOM LETCHWORTH

 **Fermata House**
www.fermatahouse.com

ISBN 978-1-947566-00-2
Library of Congress Control Number: 2017910607

Published by Fermata House: Searcy, Arkansas www.fermatahouse.com

Unless otherwise noted, Scripture quotations are taken from the Holy Bible: World English Bible. The World English Bible (WEB) is a Public Domain Modern English translation of the Holy Bible. The World English Bible is based on the American Standard Version of the Holy Bible first published in 1901, the Biblia Hebraica Stutgartensa Old Testament, and the Greek Majority Text New Testament.

Website addresses in the Notes sections were last accessed on July 4, 2017.

Cover and chapter title fonts:
   Opera-Lyrics by Dennis Bathory-Kitsz.
   Optimus Princeps by Manfred Klein.

Chapter title flags were cropped from *Map showing the battle field at Harrisburg, Miss. July 13-15, 1864* (Library of Congress, 99447417).

Cover photos:

July 4, 1862 – at Mr. James Hunter's Hestonville Pa
   For description, see Notes after Chapter 2.
   (Library of Congress, LC-DIG-stereo-1s01483)

Hospital at Fredericksburg, Va., May 1864
   Library of Congress description: Photograph shows soldiers outside a brick hospital building in Fredericksburg, Virginia, recovering from wounds received during the battles in the "Wilderness campaign." Woman seated in doorway is volunteer nurse Abby Hopper Gibbons from New York.   (Library of Congress, 2009630187)

Premade BG 94 by Brenda Clarke was used for text backgrounds.

I am eternally grateful
for that unknown Yankee soldier
who captured a Confederate Sergeant
by the name of William Letchworth.
William lay on the field, seriously wounded
in the aftermath of the Battle of Bristoe Station.
That Yankee soldier made sure he received medical care.

I must also express my appreciation for
the hospital personnel at Fairfax Seminary USA General Hospital near
Alexandria, Virginia; the Lincoln USA General Hospital in Washington
D.C.; and General Hospitals No. 9 and No. 24 in Richmond, Virginia.
These medical professionals and volunteers, both Union and Confederate,
attended to William so that he survived the war and returned home.

In memory of Sgt. William Letchworth

William LETCHWORTH volunteered for Confederate service on 11 MAR 1862 in Pitt County, North Carolina. He was enrolled as a Private in Company C, 44th North Carolina Infantry. He was promoted to 5th Sergeant, Company C sometime after February 1863 and prior to his capture on 14 OCT 1863 at Bristoe Station, Virginia. He suffered a serious flesh wound in the right hip and was treated successively at the Fairfax Seminary USA General Hospital near Alexandria, VA (15-23 OCT 63) and the Lincoln USA General Hospital in Washington, DC (23 OCT 63–8 FEB 1864). He was transferred to Old Capitol Prison in DC and held there until 15 JUN 1864 when he was forwarded to Fort Delaware arriving on 17 JUN 1864. He was selected for a "humanitarian" exchange of sick and debilitated prisoners at Fort Delaware. Paroled for exchange on 14 SEP 1864, he and others were sent away on 18 SEP 1864 and officially delivered to Confederate authorities at Varina, Virginia (aka Aikens Landing) on the north bank of the James River. He was admitted to the Receiving & Wayside Hospital (General Hospital No. 9) in Richmond for evaluation on 21 SEP 1864 and sent to General Hospital No. 24 (the Moore Hospital) on 22 SEP 1864. His name appears on a clothing issue record dated 26 SEP 1864 at the Winder General Hospital. This was usually the prelude to being released on furlough or returned to his unit.

Contents

INTRODUCTION

Why Another Book About the Civil War?

Where the past humbles us, we are reminded of our humanity; where the past inspires us, we are driven to greater things; where the past leaves wounds, we continue to seek healing. This is why, with all of its horrors and bloodshed, the Civil War still haunts the psyche of the United States of America more than 150 years later. And it may explain why you are holding this book in your hands. Perhaps you share with me a fascination with that dramatic era.

As we reflect on the political tensions that led to this divisive war, we remember those terrible battles, and the young men maimed physically and spiritually. We remember for the same reason we reflect on our own past mistakes and sins and triumphs—so that we may repent and fare forward into the future while learning from the past.

My purpose in writing this book is to reflect on spiritual insights which are inspired by unusual Civil War events. Each of these thirty devotionals merely skims the surface of the events and characters they describe. I have included footnotes at the end of each chapter as a guide for you to discover more about these wonderful stories.

My prayer is that you will see that we are all connected to the past, and that what we do in the present does have implications for the future. We are all a part of this story.

Proudly wearing a Union cap, this little guy poses with a soldier. Tom Liljenquist donated this photo to the Library of Congress in 2010. The Library staff titled it: *Unidentified soldier in Union uniform and kepi with unidentified young boy, probably father and son.*[1]

Imitation Is the Highest Form of Flattery

Civil War reenactments have become a big deal in our era. Civil War reenactors pile their tents and haversacks and Enfield rifle replicas into the back of the van and head out to places across the land where more than 150 years ago, blue and gray clad soldiers fought in deadly, desperate ferocity.

The reenactors honor the memory of these soldiers by conjuring up the smell of campfires, the choking smoke of artillery, and by lining up as the real soldiers once did for massed fire and pitched battles.

I guess in a sense I was a wannabe reenactor long ago. Even though my family's heritage was in North Carolina, Georgia and West Texas, I begged my parents for a "real" _Union_ uniform.

Believe it or not, they were available for a six-year-old in the old Sears Catalogue, and I flipped to that page and circled it and left it open by my dad's chair. I'm not saying I didn't trust Santa Claus, but I wasn't leaving anything to chance!

On Christmas morning, I was ecstatic to find a Union soldier's uniform in a package under the tree!

As I carefully put on my little uniform, buttoning my brass U.S. buttons in a deep reverie, my Grandpop, from Savannah, Georgia, teased me a bit. He said he didn't much care for the blue color—since his grandfather had fought for the Confederacy with the 44th North Carolina Regiment.

There are times that history comes alive for us. It came alive for me even then.

I remember reading about Carl Sandburg, the great American poet, who was working on his multi-volume biography of Abraham Lincoln. The story is told that Sandburg would become so engrossed in his subject that he nearly forgot what century he was in.

Some of the wags in town decided to play a prank on him. They knew the restaurant where Sandburg ate breakfast every day. So, they dressed up a Lincoln impersonator, beard and stove pipe hat and all, to stand on the street corner that Sandburg would pass.

Carl Sandburg came strolling down the street, the pranksters trying to contain their mirth. Sandburg was obviously deep in thought, and as he passed the Lincoln look-alike, he simply tipped his hat as though it was perfectly normal to see Mr. Lincoln standing there, and said, *Good morning, Mr. President.*[2]

Part of our task as Christians we are told in Scripture, is to, "Be therefore imitators of God, as beloved children. Walk in love, even as Christ also loved you, and gave himself up for us, an offering and a sacrifice to God for a sweet-smelling fragrance."[3]

Such imitation has a long, illustrious history in Christian spirituality. Thomas a Kempis wrote an entire book devoted to *The Imitation of Christ.* Charles Sheldon's book, *In His Steps*, written more than a century ago, influenced a recent generation to ask themselves the question, "What would Jesus do?"

In my own experience, imitating Christ is <u>not</u> something that I can do in my own power. I can't overcome my own frailties and fallibilities. Those rare times when I have "imitated Christ," it has been through God's grace alone.

It's all about what <u>God</u> has done <u>for</u> us and <u>in</u> us, not what we have done for ourselves.

I can't say it any better than the Apostle Paul: "I have been crucified with Christ, and it is no longer I that live, but Christ living in me. That life which I now live in the flesh, I live by faith in the Son of God, who loved me, and gave himself up for me."[4]

Our Lord, you call upon us not only to imitate you, but to live in you as you live in us. So fill me with your spiritual DNA so that when people see me, they see you. Amen.

Notes

1. *Unidentified soldier in Union uniform and kepi with unidentified young boy, probably father and son,*
(Library of Congress, 2011645301).
2. Lloyd John Ogilvie, *The Red Ember in the White Ash* (Eugene: Harvest House Publishers, 2006), 91.
3. Ephesians 5:1-2 (World English Bible).
4. Galatians 2:20 (World English Bible).

Coleman Sellers photographed this particular picnic gathering on July 4, 1862. The gathering took place at Mr. James Hunter's in Hestonville, Pennsylvania. The photo is cropped from the original stereograph which is part of the Charles F. Himes collection of stereographs by amateur photographers at the Library of Congress.[1]

2

War Ain't No Picnic

The battle was supposed to be brief and decisive. That's what everyone, including the spectators, expected when they arrived near Manassas, Virginia. Congressmen, reporters, and the generally curious traveled thirty miles west from our nation's capital, picnic baskets in tow, hoping to catch a glimpse of this *entertaining event.*

But entertainment morphed into lethal chaos as two inexperienced armies locked arms on that sweltering July day in 1861.

There were some who knew these two armies weren't ready for a real fight. General Winfield Scott, a grizzled veteran of the Mexican American War and the overall commander of the Union forces, believed that the first full year of the war should be spent in simple battle readiness—producing supplies, uniforms, weapons, and training green farm boys about real warfare.

But his opinion wasn't shared by the politicians, the lovely young women in hoop skirts waving handkerchiefs at their gallant boys in uniform, or the farm boy soldiers themselves.

Confederate Brigadier General P. G. T. Beauregard was so eager to put his troops into action, he wrote on July 8, 1861: *If I could only get the enemy to attack me . . . I would stake my reputation on the handsomest victory that could be hoped for.*[2] A little less than two weeks later, he got his wish. While Beauregard and his officers were anticipating dinner at the home of Wilmer McLean, a Union artillery unit fired a shell that crashed through the kitchen. Needless to say, dinner was cancelled.

As the battle developed, Confederate Brigadier General Barnard E. Bee Jr. was ordered to move his troops and artillery to Henry Hill. He was so certain that he was being sidelined by these orders that he was disgusted when an officer expressed concern that the troops hadn't had anything to eat. Bee snapped: *You will have plenty of time to cook and eat to the music of a battle in which we will probably take little or no part.*[3] At the end of the day, he would be mortally wounded.

Some of the good people of Washington were convinced that the war would be a lark. They followed the Union troops for the day as though they were part of a parade. They came in carriages, wagons, buggies and on horseback, well-supplied with picnic hampers and drink.

The spectators, dressed in their finery and munching on fried chicken and cucumber slices, watched the battle seesaw back and forth, like a horrifying tennis match. Most of them stayed a safe five-mile distance, where they required strong field glasses.

It may have been a little like watching a game without really knowing the rules, or recognizing the players. In many cases, the uniforms of both sides looked identical. Some of the Confederate regiments still wore the blue uniforms from their previous allegiance to the Union. The battle flags were so close in color that even General P. G. T. Beauregard, commanding the Confederate army, couldn't tell from a distance whether approaching troops were friendly or hostile.

The spectators might have cheered when the Union soldiers in blue took the top of Henry House Hill. But their elation would have been short-lived. Led by General Thomas Jackson, the Confederate Virginians retook the hill and drove the panicked Yankees down the hill and across the stream, where many of the harassed soldiers threw their rifles down.

These civilian spectators might have been among the first, along with the unseasoned Union troops, to hear the fabled "rebel yell" in battle. General Jackson had exhorted his men: *And when you charge, yell like furies!*[4]

As the battle swirled in their direction, the spectators found themselves uncomfortably involved. Picnic baskets were swept up in haste, or abandoned, as the onlookers became part of a chaotic retreat toward Washington D.C. This distinguished "audience" had expected an afternoon's diversion, and now they were running for their lives!

There is very little room today for mere *spectators*. Watching passively as others fight the battle could be dangerous. We ourselves may become casualties in the struggle between right and wrong.

Jesus speaks of the struggle between good and evil. "He who is not with me is against me, and he who doesn't gather with me, scatters."[5]

Our Lord, we know that we cannot be morally or spiritually neutral today. We cannot be merely spectators. Grant me the wisdom to know your will, and the courage to follow your will. Amen.

Notes

1. *July 4, 1862 - at Mr. James Hunter's Hestonville Pa* (Library of Congress, LC-DIG-stereo-1s01483).
2. Alfred Roman, *The Military Operations of General Beauregard* (New York, 1884), 82.
3. General John D. Imboden, "Incidents of the Battle of Manassas" *The Century Illustrated Monthly Magazine* 30 (May 1885 to October 1885): 93.
4. Craig A. Warren, *The Rebel Yell* (Tuscaloosa: The University of Alabama Press, 2014), 54.
5. Matthew 12:30 (World English Bible).

This photo of General Bee's portrait was taken during the restoration of the historic McClanahan house, the oldest business structure in Beeville, Texas. (Courtesy of the Beeville Historical Society)

Full description as listed on the University of North Texas website:

> *This portrait of Barnard E. Bee, Jr. in his military uniform hangs in the McClanahan House in Beeville. Barnard E. Bee, Jr. was the son of Anne and Barnard E. Bee, Sr. (for whom Bee County is named) and was born in Charleston, South Carolina in 1824. He moved to Texas with his family in 1836, but later returned to the east and graduated from West Point. He served with honors in the Mexican War. In 1861 he resigned from the US Army and joined the First South Carolina Regulars, a Confederate regiment of artillery. While assigned to the Army of Virginia at Manassas Junction, Bee is given credit for ordering his men to "Rally behind the Virginians! There stands Jackson like a stonewall!". He fell mortally wounded at this First Battle of Manassas, or Bull Run, and died on July 22, 1861. His body is buried at Pendleton, South Carolina. He was the brother of Texas Statesman, Hamilton Bee.*[1]

3

What's in a Name

Geneal Thomas Jackson was the artillery teacher at Virginia Military Institute. Known as a rather rigid, boring instructor, he was given the nickname *Tom Fool* by his students (behind his back, of course).[2]

On July 21, 1861, General Jackson was in command of five Confederate Virginia regiments near Manassas, Virginia, just 30 miles west of our nation's capital. They were about to be overrun by Union soldiers on Henry House Hill.

The smoke and noise from the artillery was disorienting. It was difficult to tell one side from the other. Some of the Rebel units still wore the blue uniforms of the Union regiments in which they had previously been enlisted.

There was another officer there. Brigadier General Barnard Bee, from South Carolina, was in command of the Third Brigade of the Confederate Army of the Shenandoah. General Bee saw what was about to happen, and told General Jackson: *The Enemy are driving us!*

Jackson replied: *Then, Sir, we will give them the bayonet!*

Bee exhorted his own troops to re-form, shouting: *There is Jackson, standing like a stone wall. Let us determine to die here, and we will conquer. Rally behind the Virginians!* [3]

It may well be that General Bee was the superior tactician. It may even be that he was being critical of Jackson for taking too long to advance. We'll never know. He was mortally wounded in the next moments and perished on Henry House Hill. But the legend of *Stonewall* Jackson and his Virginians was born — and they pressed on to charge and retake the hill, driving the Yankee soldiers into a disorderly retreat across Bull Run stream.

After the Battle of Manassas, *Tom Fool* became better known as *Stonewall* Jackson, one of the greatest tacticians of the Civil War, and General Robert E. Lee's most reliable General.

Some of us may be like *Stonewall* Jackson who distinguished himself as a commander. He carried the day at Manassas. He outwitted the Union army with his maneuvers in the Shenandoah Valley. He surprised the Union Army of the Potomac at Mechanicsville. He set up a decisive victory at Chancellorsville. Some of us may be distinguished and famous—some of us, not all of us.

But all of us can (and should) be like General Barnard Bee, who re-named General Thomas Jackson, freeing him to shed the *Tom Fool* moniker and adopt his new image as *Stonewall* Jackson.

All of us can serve our role in history as an ***identifier*** and ***namer***—identifying and naming the gifts we see in others, assisting them to become everything they are meant to be.

John the Baptist said of Jesus: "Behold, the Lamb of God, who takes away the sin of the world! . . . He must increase, but I must decrease."[4] John recognized the uniqueness of Jesus and also accepted that he was surpassed by Jesus. We ***identify*** and ***name***, lifting up those around us, even at the risk of our own obscurity.

I think of another example. If we are asked to identify the most famous apostle and missionary in the early church other than Peter, most of us would answer —Paul, of course. However, we might never have heard about Paul unless another Christian had spoken up on his behalf. His name was Joses, and he was a believer who was originally from the island of Cyprus. He himself had received a noble nickname because of his generosity to the early church—*Barnabas*, which means "Son of Encouragement."

When Barnabas met a young Jew named Saul, he knew by reputation that Saul had been a terror to the Christian community. Saul had been commissioned to persecute the church. But on the Road to Damascus, he was confronted by Christ. He was converted. Saul had begun to preach the Gospel, but the Christians were still very wary of him.

It was Barnabas who became an advocate for Saul and helped pave the way for his acceptance by the Apostles. And this same Saul later becomes known as *Paul*, the "Apostle to the Gentiles." Barnabas, though he "discovered" Saul, disappears into obscurity. But he had done a terrific thing for the sake of the early church in discovering and recommending Saul.

Our Lord, grant us the discernment to recognize the spiritual gifts of others, and to identify and name them as your servants. Knowing who we are in you is the key to our true identity. Amen.

Notes

1. <http://texashistory.unt.edu/ark:/67531/metapth78787/>
2. James I. Robertson, Jr., *Stonewall Jackson The Man, The Soldier, The Legend* (New York: MacMillan Publishing, 1997), 122.
3. Lieut.-Col. G. F. R. Henderson, C.B., *Stonewall Jackson and the American Civil War Vol. 1* (London: Longmans, Green, and Co., 1909), 145.
4. John 1:29b, 3:30 (World English Bible).

This photograph of chaplains serving in the 9th Corps was taken October 1864, during the siege of Petersburg, Virginia. It is part of Hirst D. Milhollen and Donald H. Mugridge's compilation of Civil War photographs at the Library of Congress.[1]

4

Disputing Theology at Gunpoint

General Jackson, the famous "Stonewall" of the Virginians, was a deeply devout Christian. He took the Ten Commandments seriously, including the fourth—"Remember the Sabbath day, to keep it holy."[2] He preferred not to fight on a Sunday if he didn't have to, although he relented as the war progressed.

But on one occasion during the campaign in the Shenandoah Valley in 1862, Jackson requisitioned gunpowder for the coming battle. He wanted to be sure, though, that it wasn't procured on the Sabbath. The quartermaster wasn't able to find the powder on Saturday, but he was successful on Sunday.

On Monday, when word came to Jackson that the powder had been acquired on Sunday, he sent another officer in search of an alternate powder. When it arrived, he tersely spoke to his subordinate officer: *Colonel, I desire that you will see that the powder which is used for this expedition is not the powder that was procured on Sunday.*[3]

When the General gives an order, there is no dispute. However, some theological doctrines were disputed during the Civil War, as was the case with a certain army chaplain.

Major Robert Dabney was a Confederate chaplain who was of a "Presbyterian" persuasion. He strongly believed in the five points of Calvinism, and hammered them home at nearly every opportunity. These five points supported the doctrine of predestination.

He was so very zealous that it could be said that every soldier in the camp knew the "Eternal Decrees" by heart—even the Methodists who knew they couldn't be right!

According to legend, the chaplain's theology was tested when his regiment happened upon a Union ambush. An unexpected firefight broke out—the minié balls flew thick as hail between the two sides.

The chaplain was caught in the midst of this violence as an unarmed noncombatant. So . . . he nimbly ducked behind a huge tree for safety.

A young private watched the chaplain's "better part of valor" with amusement. Between firing and reloading, the soldier couldn't resist the opportunity to needle the chaplain. (Perhaps the soldier was a Methodist?!)

He called out: *I thought you believed in the Eternal Decrees, Reverend! No bullet can hurt you if it's not predestined!*

The chaplain drew himself up with dignity—though still hiding behind the tree—and said: *The tree was predestined to be here, and I was predestined to run and jump behind it!* [4]

People of faith may disagree over some of the subtleties of Christian doctrine. We do well to remember a formula that can help resolve some of the unnecessary tensions: unity in the essentials; liberty in the non-essentials; love in all things.

Or, as the Apostle Paul would say: "Now accept one who is weak in faith, but not for disputes over opinions."[5]

Our Lord, there are many things your family fusses about in the church. Please remind us that though we may disagree, until that time when faith is sight, we are nonetheless family. We may not all think alike, but we can love alike. Amen.

Notes

1. *Petersburg, Va. Chaplains of the 9th Corps*
   (Library of Congress, cwp2003000584/PP).
2. Exodus 20:8 (*World English Bible*).
3. Margaret J. Preston, "Personal Reminiscences of Stonewall Jackson"
   The Century Illustrated Monthly Magazine 32 (May 1886 to October
   1886): 931.
   Margaret Junkin Preston was the wife of Major John T. L. Preston,
   who was the Colonel to whom Jackson was speaking. Margaret's
   sister, Elinor "Ellie" Junkin Jackson, was Jackson's first wife. She
   died from childbirth complications a little over a year after their
   marriage. Margaret and Ellie's father, Rev. George Junkin, was a
   leading Presbyterian theologian.
4. Though Robert Lewis Dabney actually served as a chaplain with the
   18th Virginia Infantry Regiment, his "predestined tree story" may
   well be apocryphal, as there are many versions of the story. For
   Senator Sam Ervin's version, see: Sam J. Ervin, Jr., *Humor of a
   Country Lawyer* (Chapel Hill: The University of North Carolina
   Press, 1983), 83.
   Major Dabney later served as Stonewall Jackson's chief of staff.
5. Romans 14:1 (World English Bible).

The Sixth Pennsylvania Cavalry were known as "Rush's Lancers," named after their commander, Colonel Richard Henry Rush and their nine-foot lances. This cavalry regiment was formed in the fall of 1861. Pictured here is Company I. This was photographed by Matthew Brady in Falmouth, Virginia in June 1863. The Library of Congress describes this photo: "Photograph shows 'Rush's Lancers' with Capt. J. Starr and Lt. F. Furness seated in front."[1]

5

Obsolete Weapons

In the development of military weaponry, the use of lances may have been one of the most romantic and nostalgic ideas of the Civil War, and the least practical. A politician in Pennsylvania noted that there were not enough muskets for the young men volunteering to serve in the early days of the Civil War. He had a "brilliant" idea—why not arm them with lances, like the knights described by Sir Walter Scott in his popular novels?

Driven by political pressure, Pennsylvania Governor Andrew G. Curtin lobbied the United States War Department to produce one thousand lances.[2] Each lance was nine feet long, tipped with a three-edged blade nearly a foot long. Impressive and menacing—especially when festooned with bright red banners. But not very effective against rifled muskets that could easily drop a man at half a mile. Most of the lances remained uselessly stacked in warehouses.[3]

Other weaponry that might have served a purpose in past wars was also obsolete. General Stonewall Jackson used his saber so infrequently that when he did try to rally his troops by unsheathing it and brandishing it over his head, he discovered that the saber had rusted and was stuck in the scabbard.[4]

Even bayonets were seldom used except as spits for roasting meat or as candlesticks—although there were notable exceptions. The 20th Maine Regiment, under the leadership of Union Colonel Joshua Lawrence Chamberlain, had held the crown of the Little Round Top at Gettysburg in the face of six determined Rebel assaults.

Colonel Chamberlain had been directed to hold the hill at all costs. With mounting casualties and dwindling ammunition, he ordered his men to fix bayonets on their rifles. The order went down the line like an electric current.

Chamberlain gave the command to advance, and the line of blue descended down the slope of the Little Round Top. Through a combination of great timing and dumb luck, the 358 remaining members of the 20th Maine managed to overcome at least two regiments of Confederates.[5]

When we read of weaponry in the Scriptures, we might conclude that everything mentioned there is obsolete. Swords? Shields? Breastplates? How would they fare against automatic rifles or drones and smart bombs?

We are reminded that spiritually we are protected against the flaming arrows of the Evil One by the shield of faith. As Isaiah 54:17 says, "No weapon that is formed against you will prevail." [6]

But the spiritual armor of God is always invincible: "For though we walk in the flesh, we don't wage war according to the flesh; for the weapons of our warfare are not of the flesh, but mighty before God to the throwing down of strongholds. . ."[7]

Our Lord, your Word advises us that we are engaged in spiritual warfare, and that we fight not against flesh and blood, but against demonic powers. Only weapons formed by you will ultimately be of any use—truth, righteousness, peace, faith, and salvation. Arm us with your weapons, and we will be invincible. Amen.

Notes

1. *Company I, 6th Pennsylvania Cavalry, Falmouth, Va., June 1863* (Library of Congress, 2013648496).
2. Robert P. Broadwater, *Civil War Special Forces: The Elite and Distinct Fighting Units of the Union* (Santa Barbara: Praeger, 2014), 14.
3. Eric J. Wittenberg, ed., *We Have it Damn Hard Out Here: The Civil War Letters of Sergeant Thomas W. Smith, 6th Pennsylvania Cavalry* (Kent: The Kent State University Press, 1999), 3-4.
4. Thomas R. Flagel, *The History Buff's Guide to the Civil War* (Naperville: Cumberland House, 2010), 91.
5. Report of Colonel Joshua L. Chamberlain, July 6, 1863, U.S War Department, *The War of the Rebellion: A Compilation of the Official Records of the Union and Confederate Armies*, series 1, vol. 27, part I, 624.
6. Isaiah 54:17 (World English Bible).
7. 2 Corinthians 10:3-4 (World English Bible).

Seeking for the wounded, by torch-light, after the battle appeared in the March 8, 1862 issue of *Harper's Weekly.* Though the drawing refers specifically to the Battle of Fort Donelson, it illustrates how soldiers searched for wounded men after a battle.[1]

6

Glow in the Dark Wounds

Than are eerie tales that emerge from Civil War battlefields. Tales of ghosts that still walk the battlefields, seeking rest. Understandable, given the intensely violent nature of war.

My wife and I visited a military park that played a somewhat minor role in one of Sherman's advances. But no battle or skirmish was ever minor to those who were wounded, or worse, lost their lives in such an encounter.

The park interpreter, an older gentleman who loved the lore of the battlefield, explained how the battle had played out, and why it was of at least some importance in the campaign. But he also touched on some of the more "supernatural" effects of the aftermath of the battle.

He told us that from time to time, some visitors have seen the figure of a young Rebel flitting through the shade of the ancient trees in the fading afternoon light.

And he told us that one day, on a clear afternoon just before sunset, he and his brother-in-law were sitting on his porch just a few miles away from the battlefield when they both heard the undeniable report of artillery fire, booming from the direction of the battlefield. He assured us there wasn't a cloud in the sky, so it couldn't have been thunder. And there were no modern Army bases anywhere nearby. All he and his brother-in-law could do was stare at each other.

Of course, there are probably ghost stories about nearly every battlefield in the Civil War. The grief for more than 620,000 Johnny Rebs or Billy Yanks who fell in battle, or died of dysentery in camps certainly created a longing for some kind of connection with the dead. Especially for those whose faith in the promises of the Gospel was shaken.

Frankly, I'm of the skeptical school of thought that would require some fairly good evidence before I buy into the paranormal phenomena.

But what of the eerie tale of glowing wounds from the terrible Battle of Shiloh, Tennessee? This battle was still fairly early in the war—April 1862. More than 16,000 soldiers from both sides were wounded Some of the wounded lay in the field overnight. Others were left for as long as two rain-soaked days.

When litter bearers came to pick up these groaning, bleeding men, they noticed something that seemed unearthly—in many cases their wounds glowed in the dark! Even more strangely, those with glowing wounds seemed to heal more effectively than others!

Naturally, this phenomenon was dismissed by most reasonable people—until 2001.

Bill Martin, a Maryland High School student, heard this "apocryphal" tale during a visit to the Shiloh Battlefield. He got curious. When he returned home, he had a conversation with his mother—a microbiologist at the USDA Agricultural Research Service. He asked her about some of her work on a bacterium that happened to be her specialty—*Photohabdus luminescens*. This is a bacterium which inhibits pathogenic infections. And under certain conditions, it glows in the dark![2]

Bill and his friend, Jonathan Curtis, researched this phenomenon and submitted their findings at an international science fair, which they won. They had discovered that this glow-in-the-dark bacteria grows in the kind of hypothermic conditions that soldiers might well have experienced on that damp April battlefield. Not only did their wounds glow in the dark, they also healed more quickly.[3]

There is a Light that provides ultimate healing and cleansing. It is the light of Christ: "But if we walk in the light, as he is in the light, we have fellowship with one another, and the blood of Jesus Christ, his Son, cleanses us from all sin."[4]

Our Lord, we are all wounded in one way or another. May your cleansing and healing Light bring wholeness to our lives. Amen.

Notes

1. *Seeking for the wounded, by torch-light, after the battle* (Library of Congress, 2004669212) This is an illustration from *Harper's Weekly*, v. 6, no. 271 (1862 March 8), p. 149. Full description as listed on the Library of Congress website: *Print shows soldiers searching by torch-light through a wooded area for wounded soldiers after a Rebel assault on Schwartz's battery during the Union siege of Fort Donelson, Tennessee.*
2. Sharon Durham, "Students May Have Answer for Faster-Healing Civil War Wounds that Glowed" *United States Department of Agriculture: Agricultural Research Service*, May 29, 2001. <https://www.ars.usda.gov/news-events/news/research-news/2001/students-may-have-answer-for-faster-healing-civil-war-wounds-that-glowed/>
3. "Glowing Wounds" *Science Updates* podcast. *American Association for the Advancement of Science.* < http://sciencenetlinks.com/science-news/science-updates/glowing-wounds/>
4. 1 John 1:7 (World English Bible).

Mary Ann Bickerdyke was a widow when the Civil War erupted. She volunteered as a nurse and hospital administrator for the Union, and earned the affectionate nickname *Mother Bickerdyke* from the troops. She served in many of the major military battles of the Western Theater during the war.[1]

She Ranks Me

Where does real authority come from? In the Civil War, there was a chain of command for both armies, and authority flowed down from above, beginning with the commander in chief, to the generals, colonels, captains, and so on.

But sometimes the "brass" didn't have as much authority as they thought they did.

There was a Chief of Nursing named Mary Ann Bickerdyke, known to thousands of wounded men as *Mother Bickerdyke*, who was no respecter of rank or prestige when it came to providing proper care for the ordinary soldier.

She frequently flouted military rules and regulations. She was known to offer sharp words for officers who failed to care for their men.

When General Sherman received complaints from his staff about her insubordination and disregard for military protocol, Sherman shrugged and said, *I can't help you. She has more power than I—she ranks me.*[2]

Where did such authority come from? She had no title or rank in the military. She was a woman in a man's world. She was a widow. What caused Sherman, a ferocious warrior, the scourge of Georgia, to acknowledge that he was powerless in her presence?

Mother Bickerdyke earned her authority. When she entered the military encampment at Cairo near the beginning of the war, it might be said that she *attacked* it—the way a general might attack his foes. She went through the camp and immediately began to make corrections and improve conditions.

In many ways, she was ahead of her time. She saw filth everywhere. So, she set about to sterilize and clean the tents. She threw out the dirty straw on which wounded soldiers had bled. Barrels were provided so that the men could bathe. Clean clothes were provided from the laundries that she established.

She had been an advocate of herbs and good nutrition for many years, and she cooked soups over roaring fires, and baked bread, provided eggs, fresh milk, fresh vegetables.

When the army moved out from Cairo, Mary Ann Bickerdyke moved out with the troops, and suffered the same privations and the same conditions that the soldiers did.

But what would she have said was her real source of authority?

When a disgruntled surgeon asked on what authority she was doing all that she did, she responded, *I have received my authority from the Lord God Almighty; have you anything that ranks higher than that?* [3]

There is no higher authority than that!

Jesus faced the same questions about his own authority. Like Mary Ann Bickerdyke, he demonstrated his authority by his actions. When the imprisoned John the Baptist sent messengers to Jesus, they asked: "'Are you he who comes, or should we look for another?' Jesus answered them, 'Go and tell John the things which you hear and see: the blind receive their sight, the lame walk, the lepers are cleansed, the deaf hear, the dead are raised up, and the poor have good news preached to them. Blessed is he who finds no occasion for stumbling in me.'"[4]

And Jesus also claims his own intrinsic authority: "Jesus came to them and spoke to them, saying, 'All authority has been given to me in heaven and on earth.'"[5]

And then he imparts his authority to those who would follow him: "Go, and make disciples of all nations, baptizing them in the name of the Father and of the Son and of the Holy Spirit, teaching them to observe all things that I commanded you. Behold, I am with you always, even to the end of the age."[6]

So, if we are to follow the example of Mary Ann Bickerdyke, our authority comes from the Lord God Almighty and from serving, sharing, healing and witnessing as Jesus commissions us to do.

Our Lord, you have given us authority to share your good news, to bring healing and comfort, and to be your representatives in the world. As you give us this authority, also give us the power to fulfill all that you have commanded us to do. Amen.

Notes

1. *Mother Mary Ann Ball Bickerdyke* (Library of Congress, 2002707877)
2. Mary A. Livermore, *My Story of the War: A Woman's Narrative of Four Years Personal Experience as Nurse in the Union Army, and in Relief Work at Home, in Hospitals, Camps, and at the Front, during the War of the Rebellion* (Hartford: A.D. Worthington and Company, 1889), 511.
3. Ibid., 490.
4. Matthew 11:3-6 (World English Bible).
5. Matthew 28:18 (World English Bible).
6. Matthew 28:19-20 (World English Bible).

Women supported the war effort in a variety of tasks, wherever needed. In the top panel we see women working in an arsenal during the war. *Filling cartridges at the United States Arsenal at Watertown, Massachusetts* appeared on the cover of the July 20, 1861 issue of *Harper's Weekly*.[1]

8

Women at War

We cannot overestimate the importance of women during the Civil War. Women were nurses who entered a man's world in the surgeries and the hospitals. Dorothea Dix organized a nursing corps to assist the doctors who amputated and cauterized and cared for the wounded. Clara Barton became one of the most famous of nurses. Even Louisa May Alcott, famous for writing the novel *Little Women*, volunteered as a nurse.

Dorothea Dix tried to "demystify" the women who served as nurses. In the early years of the war, she made it clear that she would not accept women who were too young or too pretty. She didn't want them "distracting" the soldiers.[2]

Women also participated in the war effort in other ways. Many women helped assemble the armaments that were to be used in battle. Other women gathered in homes and tore up old dresses for bandages. There were also tales of women who actually fought alongside their brothers and husbands, invariably disguised as boys in uniform.

One woman who found herself in a tight spot managed to extricate herself heroically by outwitting her adversaries. When the crew of the Confederate raiding schooner, the *Retribution,* captured the northern brigantine *J.P. Ellicott,* the *Ellicott's* crew members were removed and replaced by Confederate pirates. But a Union sympathizer was left on board—the wife of the *Ellicott's* first mate.

She was resourceful. She offered the store of rum to her captors. And, sailors being sailors, they soon became stuporously drunk.

While they slept off their binge, she clapped them in irons! And single-handedly she sailed the brig into the harbor of St. Thomas in the Virgin Islands, where she turned them over to Union authorities![3]

She reminds me of one woman in the Scriptures who took matters into her own hands. Deborah, of course, in the Book of Judges became the leader of the Israelites when they were oppressed by the Canaanites. We have no idea <u>how</u> she became the judge of her people in a very male-dominated era, but she must certainly have been a person of extraordinary gifts. She is called a "prophetess" in the book of Judges.[4]

When Deborah summons a warrior named Barak to lead ten thousand men against the Canaanites, he insists that she go with the army—like an ancient Joan of Arc! Her answer is interesting. She says: "I will surely go with you. Nevertheless, the journey that you take won't be for your honor; for Yahweh will sell Sisera (the warlord of the Canaanites) into a woman's hand."[5] And that is exactly what happens. The Canaanite army, with its state-of-the-art chariots of iron, are thoroughly defeated by the Israelites.

Jael was the woman who struck the decisive blow. She was the wife of Heber the Kenite. Jael pretended to offer hospitality and refuge to Sisera, the Canaanite general, as he fled from the battle. She hid Sisera in her tent, gave him milk to drink, and covered him with rugs to hide him while he slept from exhaustion—and then killed him while he slept![6]

Women are also called upon to serve in the Kingdom of God. In his sermon on the Day of Pentecost, Peter quotes the prophecy of Joel: "It will be in the last days, says God, that I will pour out my Spirit on all flesh. Your sons and your daughters will prophesy. Your young men will see visions. Your old men will dream dreams."[7]

In God's economy, men and women alike are called upon to serve.

Lord, we thank you for the men and women who make a difference in our world. We thank you that you are no respecter of persons, and that all of us can find an active role in your kingdom. Amen.

Notes

1. *Filling cartridges at the United States Arsenal at Watertown, Massachusetts* (Library of Congress, 98507937). This is an illustration from *Harper's weekly*, v. 5, 1861 July 20, p. 449 (cover). Full description as listed on the Library of Congress website: *Illustration showing women seated around a table filling cartridges and view below of four men inserting powder.*
2. *Circular No. 8 Regarding Requirements for Female Nursing Applicants, 7/14/1862* (National Archives Catalog). <https://catalog.archives.gov/id/3819334>
3. "A Heroine.; RECAPTURE OF THE BRIG. J. P. ELLICOTT FROM A REBEL PRIZE CREW," *New York Times* (New York, NY), March 1, 1863; Webb Garrison, *Civil War Stories: Strange Tales, Oddities, Events & Coincidences* (New York: Promontory Press, 1997), 44.
4. Judges 4.
5. Judges 4:9 (World English Bible).
6. Judges 4:17-21.
7. Acts 2:17 (World English Bible) Peter quotes Joel 2:28.

WAR AIN'T NO PICNIC

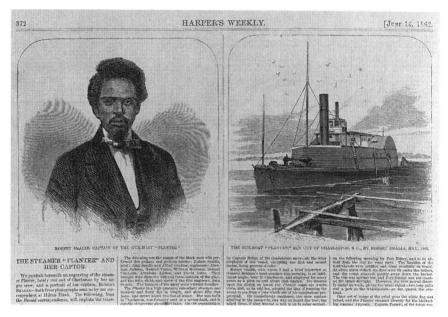

Harper's Weekly published an account of Robert Small's daring escape from slavery in its June 14, 1862 issue. The beginning of the article reads as follows:

> We publish herewith an engraving of the steamer Planter, lately run out of Charleston by her negro crew, and a portrait of her captain, ROBERT SMALLS—both from photographs sent us by our correspondent at Hilton Head. The following, from the Herald correspondence, will explain the transaction: One of the most daring and heroic adventures since the war commenced was undertaken and successfully accomplished by a party of negroes in Charleston on Monday night last.[1]

Robert Smalls went on to a distinguished career. He helped persuade President Lincoln to permit full inclusion of African Americans in the Union military. He also served as a Union Navy captain himself during the war. Following the war, Smalls became a successful businessman in Charleston and a politician. He was elected to both the South Carolina House of Representatives and the State Senate, and also served in the United States House of Representatives.

9

Sailing Home to Freedom

Frederick Douglass, the eloquent former slave who advocated for abolition, is widely quoted as saying: *I prayed for freedom for twenty years, but received no answer until I prayed with my legs.*

Robert Smalls found freedom a different way. He sailed to freedom.

As a trusted slave in Charleston, South Carolina, Robert was hired out as a source of income for his master. He was a hard worker. Resourceful. Intelligent. And he longed to be free.

His diligence earned him the right to pilot boats through the Charleston Harbor and the rivers nearby. He was highly trusted. But he was still a slave.

In the fall of 1861, Smalls worked on the *CSS Planter*—a Confederate military vessel whose crew consisted of three white Confederate officers and five slave crewmembers. As the pilot, Smalls would have seen Union ships as they lay just seven miles out from Charleston, where they blockaded the harbor.

Working in collusion with the other slave crewmen, Robert Smalls conceived a daring plan to gain their freedom. On May 12, 1862, the *Planter* sailed to a Confederate post southwest of Charleston. The *Planter's* mission was to transport four cannons and 200 pounds of ammunition back to Fort Ripley. On the way to Fort Ripley, the boat docked in its usual berth in Charleston for the night.

That night, the three white Confederate officers disembarked from the *Planter* in order to spend the evening in the city. Robert Smalls and his crew remained on board.

In the dark hours of the morning, Smalls donned the uniform of the ship's captain and put on a straw hat like the one the captain typically wore. He then quietly ordered the slave crew to cast off. As previously arranged, they stopped at a nearby wharf to pick up his own family and the families of the other crewmen! As they sailed from the wharf, Robert prayed: *Oh Lord, we entrust ourselves into thy hands. Like thou didst for the Israelites in Egypt, please stand guard over us and guide us to our promised land of freedom.*[2]

The *Planter* passed the various Confederate harbor forts without raising an alarm. Once past Confederate waters, they sailed toward the Union fleet, replacing the Confederate flag with a white sheet as a sign of surrender. The Union captain of the *USS Onward* boarded the *CSS Planter*. Smalls asked the captain for a new flag to replace his white sheet—the flag of the United States of America.

Robert Smalls' feat was the first of many contributions to his nation. His experience as a Confederate ship's pilot and his intimate knowledge of the Charleston harbor were invaluable to the U.S. Navy. He later lobbied President Lincoln to permit freed slaves to enlist in the U.S. military so that they too might join in the fight for freedom.[3]

When men and women are committed to freedom, they are interested not only in their own freedom but the freedom of all people.

Freedom is woven into the very fiber of the Bible. One of its central themes is liberation and deliverance:

- God liberates the people of Israel from the bondage of slavery in Egypt.[4] This pattern occurs again and again throughout the Old Testament, as God continues to deliver them from the oppression of their enemies.
- The message of freedom from the bondage of sin and death permeates the New Testament.

Jesus makes this promise to all who follow him: "If you remain in my word, then you are truly my disciples. You will know the truth, and the truth will make you free ... If therefore the Son makes you free, you will be free indeed."[5]

This is the ultimate freedom.

Our Lord, the chains of bondage and slavery that most of us face today are more ambiguous than the slavery of the Old South. Our slavery is to addiction, materialism, consumerism, lust, and a host of other "masters and mistresses." As Robert Smalls found freedom by sailing away from slavery and toward his liberators, may we find freedom as we turn away from sin and seek you, the ultimate Liberator. Amen.

Notes

1. "The Steamer 'Planter' and Her Captor" *Harper's Weekly* vol. 6, no. 285 (June 14, 1862): 372. (Also Library of Congress, 97512451).
2. Okon Edet Uya *From Slavery to Public Service: Robert Smalls, 1839-1915* (New York: Oxford University Press, 1971), 15.
3. Patrick Brennan *Secessionville: Assault on Charleston* (Campbell: Savas, 1996), 20-27.
   To learn more about the life of Robert Smalls, see: "The Audacity of Robert Smalls | Michael B. Moore | TEDxStMarksSchool" where Michael Boulware Moore talks about the legacy of his great-great-grandfather, Robert Smalls. The video was published on Nov. 6, 2015. <https://www.youtube.com/watch?v=w6T7ksyhUkw>
4. Exodus chapters 3 to 15.
5. John 8:31-32, 36 (World English Bible).

The Library of Congress' collection of Abraham Lincoln Papers includes his memorandum on Gabriel R. Paul, written August 23, 1862. The Lincoln Studies Center at Knox College transcribed the correspondence:

> *To-day, Mrs. Major Paul, of the Regular Army calls and urges the appointment of her husband as a Brig–Genl. She is a saucy woman and I am afraid she will keep tormenting till I may have to do it.*[1]

Doesn't Hurt to Ask

Intercession on behalf of another can be a powerful force. Lieutenant Colonel Gabriel R. Paul had been promoted to Colonel of the 4th New Mexico Volunteers fighting on behalf of the Union against a Confederate invasion of New Mexico in 1862. He was in command of Fort Union during this period. However, when the crisis was over and the Confederates were beaten back from New Mexico, the enlistments of his men expired. And Colonel Paul was returned to his former rank as lieutenant colonel.[2]

Night after night, Lieutenant Colonel Paul and his wife grumbled about the flaws in the seniority system of the U.S. Army. And Mrs. Paul resolved to do something about it!

Louise Rodgers Paul was a determined, tenacious woman. She made the arduous journey from Fort Union, New Mexico to Washington D.C. in order to intercede for her husband with President Lincoln.

Evidently she was relentless, for Lincoln said of her after their appointment on August 23, 1862: *She is a saucy woman and I am afraid she will keep tormenting me till I may have to do it.*

Gabriel R. Paul's name was presented for promotion to brigadier general, and he was finally confirmed in April 1863.[3]

This may remind us of the parable Jesus tells of the persistent widow who wears down the obstinate and unjust judge with her pleas for justice. The unjust judge finally relents, if only to be rid of her. Jesus makes the point that God is just and merciful, and how much more is he willing to hear the prayers of those who petition him and do not lose heart?[4]

But there are even more powerful intercessors than those who are merely tenacious and persistent.

Tad Lincoln was the youngest of the Lincoln children. He had his own special code for entering his father's office—three quick taps and two slow bangs—then he entered at will, even when his father was engaged in cabinet meetings. This was a source of chagrin for the pompous Secretaries of War and of the Treasury, no doubt, but a source of merriment for Lincoln.

And Tad was known to intercede with his father. On one occasion, a delegation of citizens from Kentucky had been cooling their heels, waiting for an audience with the President. Young Tad met these men, who happened to hail from the same native state as his parents, and he decided to take matters into his own hands. No doubt employing his unique signature knock, he gained admittance to his father's office, and introduced his new friends to his *Papa-day*. As it turned out, President Lincoln had been avoiding meeting with this delegation for a week![5]

And on April 11, 1865, after Lee's surrender to Grant at Appomattox Court House, an excited crowd called for the President to come to the upper window of the White House. As he read the pages of his speech, illuminated by a candle held by newspaperman Noah Brooks, Lincoln allowed each page to drop to the floor as he finished reading it. Tad snatched them up as they fell.

When Tad heard a zealous supporter of the Union cry out that the Rebels should be hung, Tad declared: *Oh, no, we must hang on to them.* Lincoln responded, *That's right, Tad, we must hang on to them.*[6]

Jesus is the ultimate intercessor. Hebrews says that Jesus is our sinless, perfect high priest: "Therefore he is also able to save to the uttermost those who draw near to God through him, seeing that he lives forever to make intercession for them."[7]

Tad Lincoln may have had some pull with his *Papa-day*. But Jesus, who is one with the Father in the unity of the Trinity, is the Son of God. His intercessions never fail.

Our Lord, thank you that we have a peerless Intercessor. No matter what we may experience, we know that you are our Advocate. Amen.

Notes

1. The Abraham Lincoln Papers at the Library of Congress: Series 1. General Correspondence. 1833-1916. *Abraham Lincoln, Saturday, August 23, 1862 (Memorandum on Gabriel R. Paul)* (Library of Congress).
2. George W. Cullum, *Biographical Register of the Officers and Graduates of the U.S. Military Academy at West Point, N.Y., from its Establishment, March 16, 1802 to the Army Re-organization of 1866-67, 2nd Edition., Vol. 1* (New York: D. Van Nostrand, 1868), 452.
3. Park Ranger John Hoptak, "'Great in heart and mighty in valor' – General Gabriel Paul and his Mortal Wounding at Gettysburg" *From the Fields of Gettysburg (the official blog of Gettysburg National Park)*, July 10, 2014. <https://npsgnmp.wordpress.com/2014/07/10/great-in-heart-and-mighty-in-valor-general-gabriel-paul-and-his-mortal-wounding-at-gettysburg/ >
4. Luke 18:1-8.
5. Ward Hill Lamon, *Recollections of Abraham Lincoln* (Chicago: A.C. McClurg and Company, 1895), 165-166.
6. Janet Jennings, "Incidents Recalled in Washington. Recollections of Ex-Secretary McCulloch and Mrs. McCulloch and Judge Shellabarger," *Independent* (New York, NY), April 4, 1895.
7. Hebrews 7:25 (World English Bible).

On August 30, 1862, Mt. Zion Christian Church was designated as a field hospital during the Battle of Richmond, Kentucky. The photograph above shows the window that offered light and ventilation for the make-shift surgical table. As surgeons amputated limbs from wounded soldiers, they threw them out this same window. The pile of accumulated limbs reached as high as the window sill.[1]

11

The Church Is a Hospital for Sinners
...and Soldiers

Τhe south wall of Mt. Zion Christian Church in Richmond, Kentucky, still bears the scars of Rebel artillery. But to a modern visitor, the interior of the church yields a sense of serenity. And then one stops to imagine late August 1862.

It began with a skirmish. Confederate cavalry blundered into a Union picket line. This was the way so many battles seemed to begin— almost accidentally.

The next day, the Battle of Richmond began in deadly earnest. Confederate General Patrick Cleburne's troops swept toward the Union lines near Mt. Zion Christian Church—a symbol of peace in the eye of the storm.

At one point, the church became the focus of attack. Rebel forces advanced against the Union lines that had formed near those sacred grounds. The firefight was ferocious and deadly during those moments. Casualties were high. Even General Cleburne himself was hit.

Captain Irving A. Buck recalls when Cleburne was wounded:

Cleburne then rode back to give personal attention to the advance of Hill's brigade and the two batteries of Douglas and Martin. Stopping to reply to a question of Colonel Polk's, who, wounded, was being

carried to the rear, a rifle ball entered Cleburne's left cheek, carrying
away his teeth on that side, and emerging through his mouth, which,
fortunately, happened to be open in speaking to Polk.[2]

Miraculously, Cleburne's wound wasn't fatal, and after some primary care on the battlefield and a few weeks of recovery, he returned to action.

By the end of the day, a yellow flag hung over the front door of the church, marking it as neutral ground. Mt. Zion Christian Church had become a field hospital.

Mt. Zion served its purpose well as a field hospital. At first, the litters of the wounded and dying were carried into the red brick church. The litter-bearers laid these young men gently in the pews. But soon there were so many wounded that some of the litters were placed on the floor of the church, and some spilled out into the churchyard. The surgeons worked at tables in the front corner of the church building, where they sawed off limbs and searched for minié balls embedded in flesh. They operated near an open window that offered light and air— and through which they tossed amputated limbs. The discarded limbs were soon piled up all the way to the window sill outside.[3]

Today, a sensitive and imaginative soul can see the blood that washed the floor, and hear the screams of the wounded.

But where else should these agonies have been assuaged than in the house of God? This is the place where Christians had heard sermons about the passion of Christ. This is the place where Christians had received the sacred supper that signified Christ's body and blood.

Here in this place of prayer, Christ, the healer of soul and body, became incarnate in the bloody hands of surgeons.

There is an old cliché that seems to apply to what happened at Mt. Zion that day. *The church is a hospital for sinners, not a museum for saints.*

In this case, the church literally became a hospital, in which wounded soldiers wearing both blue and gray received care and prayer. Local doctors and members of the community assisted military surgeons. At their very best, these ministers of mercy didn't see Federal or Confederate soldiers—they saw suffering young men who had mothers and wives and family at home.

The church is at its best when its members love impartially: "But the wisdom that is from above is first pure, then peaceful, gentle, reasonable, full of mercy and good fruits, without partiality, and without hypocrisy. Now the fruit of righteousness is sown in peace by those who make peace."[4]

Our Lord, may our churches be hospitals for wounded souls, not museums for the relics of plaster saints. Amen.

Notes

1. Mt. Zion Christian Church in Richmond, Kentucky. Photos taken by the author August 2016. A church member serving as a docent during the reenactment of the Battle of Richmond relayed this story.
2. Irving A. Buck, *Cleburne and His Command* (New York: The Neale Publishing Company, 1908), 61.
3. The interpretive signs in the church yard and the guided tour during the 2016 Battle of Richmond Reenactment offered a wealth of information about the church's role in the Battle of Richmond; Battle of Richmond Association, "Mt. Zion Church," Battle of Richmond.org, 2012.
   < http://battleofrichmond.org/mt-zion-church/4567858399>
4. James 3:17-18 (World English Bible).

Union General Don Carlos Buell and his military career were victims of *The Acoustic Shadow* at the Battle of Perryville, in October 1862.[1]

12

Did You Hear Something?

General Braxton Bragg's Confederate troops were thirsty. They were in Kentucky in the Fall of 1862, attempting to draw Kentucky recruits into the Confederacy with a few timely victories.

They had already experienced several key victories. They had whipped the Yankees at Richmond, and had even briefly occupied the state capital in Frankfort.

But now they were desperately thirsty in a season of drought. They needed to water their horses and their troops.

Near Perryville, they encountered some small stagnant pools. They also encountered General Don Carlos Buell's Union army. Like so many battles, no one planned on fighting at this particular spot. But this battle was about water rights. The Rebels had it, and the Yankees wanted it.

And here they met on October 8, 1862—about 20,000 Union soldiers against 16,800 Confederates. It was the largest battle fought in Kentucky, and one of the bloodiest in the war. Between the two sides, there were 7,621 casualties.

The fighting was as intense as any encountered in the war. Though the Rebels were outgunned and outnumbered, they won a tactical victory on the field, pushing Union forces up ridges and slopes that were slippery with blood.

That's why the Rebel troops were shocked when they received the order to withdraw from the field. They were sure they had struck a decisive blow in the battle for Kentucky.

What they didn't know is that General Buell had another 40,000 Union troops in reserve that hadn't been thrown into action during the battle that day. The reason these troops didn't engage is among the strangest phenomena of the war. General Buell didn't even know there was a battle going on!

This wasn't because he was clueless or derelict in his duty. Because of a westerly breeze and the configuration of the Kentucky hills, there was an atmospheric phenomenon called an "acoustic shadow" that seemed to refract the sound waves from the musket fire, and most of the artillery.[2]

General Buell, recovering from a nasty fall from his horse the day before, was sitting down to a good meal. When he heard the boom of a few cannon, Buell assumed that it was a mere skirmish, or even an artillery drill.

Had he known that a major battle was occurring just over the ridge he likely would have ordered his reserve troops into action and overwhelmed Braxton Bragg's army. This might have profoundly impaired the ability of the Confederate resistance to wage war in the Western theater. Instead, Bragg was able to withdraw his troops and live to fight another day.[3]

All because of a lack of hearing.

We are reminded in Scripture that hearing is crucial. Jesus explains the resistance to his message by describing the unwillingness that some people had to hear the truth. But to those who are willing to hear the truth, he says: "... blessed are your eyes, for they see; and your ears, for they hear. For most certainly I tell you that many prophets and righteous men desired to see the things which you see, and didn't see them; and to hear the things which you hear, and didn't hear them."[4]

Lord, open my ears that I may hear your Word; and give me the will to obey what I hear. Amen.

Notes

1. *Don Carlos Buell, 1818 to 1898.* (Library of Congress, 2002709873).
2. Physics professor Dr. Charles D. Ross is an expert on the subject of acoustic shadows. He has devoted an entire book to the effect of acoustic shadows on the outcome of the Civil War.
   Charles D. Ross, *Civil War Acoustic Shadows* (Shippensburg: White Mane Pub. Co., 2001).
   One of his lectures is posted on the Civil War Museum's youtube channel: "The Tredegar Society Presents- Civil War Acoustic Shadows." <https://www.youtube.com/watch?v=VPZdzTRnuQ8>
3. Kenneth Noe, *Perryville: This Grand Havoc of Battle* (Lexington: University Press of Kentucky, 2001), 214-215, 315.
4. Matthew 13:16-17 (World English Bible).

This pencil drawing by Alfred Rudolph Waud was created December 11, 1862. He wrote the title at the bottom: *Building Pontoon Bridges at Fredericksburg Dec. 11th*. The Library of Congress describes this drawing as "Engineers in foreground constructing bridge, while Fredericksburg burns in background."[1]

13

Bridging the Gap

The Virginia rains in late November 1862 were torrential. Dirt roads turned to mud, and then to rivers. Rivers became floods.

A very reluctant General Ambrose Burnside had been ordered to take command of the Union Army of the Potomac. His good friend, General George McClellan, had been relieved of command because of President Lincoln's frustration that McClellan just wouldn't fight.

And now Burnside found himself pressured to get a win at Fredericksburg. But the bridges over the Rappahannock River had been destroyed by the Rebels.

No problem. The army engineers had pontoons that they could put across the swift Rappahannock and get Burnside's Army across the river. Then they could occupy Fredericksburg and move on to attack Lee's Army of Northern Virginia while he was still out in the open and vulnerable. The ultimate objective was to capture the "holy grail"—the Confederate capital in Richmond.

But the pontoons didn't come. Burnside's men waited. And they waited. And they waited. Various parts of the pontoon bridges were stuck in logistical limbo, typical military red tape, and even stuck (literally) in the mud.

WAR AIN'T NO PICNIC

In the meantime, General Lee's army arrived on the other side of the Rappahannock River. While the Union army waited for their pontoon bridges, the Rebels had ample time to turn Marye's Heights, overlooking Fredericksburg, into a virtual fortress. They "dug in," crouching behind a four-foot tall stone wall, which they reinforced with log breastworks and spiny abatis. And they waited for Burnside's army.

When the pontoon bridges finally arrived, they were installed with great difficulty—a rushing Rappahannock River, and Rebel sharpshooters picking off many of the Union engineers. By December 12, the Union army was finally able to cross over into Fredericksburg. From there they staged an assault on Marye's Heights.

It was a slaughter. One of the most one-sided battles of the war. Brave lines of blue-clad Union soldiers climbed the slope up Marye's Heights, only to be mowed down by Confederate rifles. Six times the lines of blue surged forward, only to be mauled by massed fire and artillery.

So horrific was the killing that Lee himself was heard to say: *It is good that war is so terrible, otherwise we would come to love it too much.*[2]

General Burnside, so distressed at the loss of the soldiers under his command, proposed to personally lead a final assault the next day, but his subordinate officers dissuaded him. Too many Union soldiers already lay dead on that hill.

If only the bridges had arrived earlier, Burnside's forces might have had a chance of fighting Lee in an open field. If only the bridges had arrived before Lee fortified Marye's Heights, Burnside's superior numbers and weaponry might have been a decisive advantage. If only.[3]

There is another bridge that is more crucial. A bridge that is dedicated to peace and salvation, not to war. A bridge that is never late.

Jesus is sometimes referred to as the "bridge" between ourselves and God the Father. This is his promise to us when he says: "I am the way, the truth, and the life. No one comes to the Father, except through me."[4]

But there is also a warning with this promise of being *the way:* "Enter in by the narrow gate; for wide is the gate and broad is the way that leads to destruction, and many are those who enter in by it. How narrow is the gate, and restricted is the way that leads to life! Few are those who find it."[5]

Our Lord, we thank you that you have bridged the abyss that exists between ourselves and you. We thank you that you have established that bridge in the fullness of time, before we even knew we needed to cross over the abyss. Enable us, by faith, to cross over to you. Amen.

Notes

1. *Building pontoon bridges at Fredericksburg Dec. 11th.* (Library of Congress, 2004660225).
2. John Esten Cooke, *A Life of General Robert E. Lee* (New York: D. Appleton and Company, 1871), 184.
3. Bruce Catton tells the story in great detail: Bruce Catton, *Bruce Catton's Civil War: Glory Road* (New York: Fairfax Press, 1984), 233-258.
4. John 14:6 (World English Bible).
5. Matthew 7:13-14 (World English Bible).

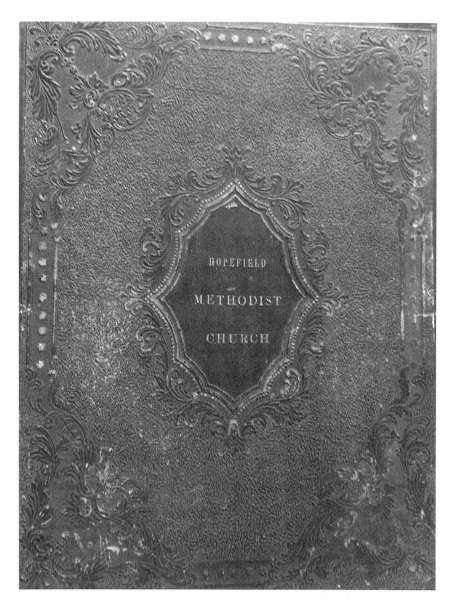

When the Federal troops gave the citizens of Hopefield one hour's warning before torching their town, Mary Jane Fulkerson (along with her mother and sister) rescued this pulpit Bible from the Hopefield Methodist Episcopal Church, South. Mrs. Fulkerson, who lived to be 102 years old, gave the Bible to her foster grandson, Jim Fullwood. His family donated it to the Crittenden County Museum.[1]

In Case of Fire ...
What Would You Save?

It is a hypothetical question that might be asked in a Sunday School class or a support group. It is intended to help folks examine their priorities: "If your house were on fire and you only had time to get one thing, what would it be?"

Three women in Hopefield, Arkansas in February 1863, had to answer that question and answer it decisively.

Their small town, on the shores of the Mississippi River opposite Memphis, Tennessee, was suspected by the blue-clad Union soldiers of harboring Confederate guerrillas. Boats from the town, these soldiers were sure, were being used up and down the river for acts of sabotage.

Memphis had been in Federal hands since the brief gunboat battle of June 6, 1862. But Captain James H. McGehee's Arkansas cavalry had attacked Union boats, coal barges and steamboats ever since.

Union Major General Stephen A. Hurlbut had had enough on February 17, 1863 when the *Hercules* was attacked just offshore at Hopefield. The tug was captured and burned, along with several coal barges.

Hurlbut ordered Union troops on February 19 to cross the river and burn this small, suspected refuge for guerrillas.

Captain Lemon, in charge of this detail, gave the citizens of Hopefield just one hour's warning before their village would be set to the torch. One can only imagine the civilians pleading with the officers and infantry, the frantic scurry to gather up some essentials from their homes. Perhaps some were paralyzed by a sense of disbelief. Perhaps they hoped that surely civility or compassion might stay the hand of the Union solders.

But sure enough, in one hour the small white houses with green shutters, the livery stable, the train depot, and the stores were all in flames. Even the Hopefield Methodist Episcopal Church, South was not spared.[2]

One can only imagine the consternation of the three women who fretted about what needed to be preserved, especially when they became convinced that these soldiers meant business. They knew at least one precious item needed to be saved—the pulpit Bible.

So, the question is raised again: "What one essential item might you save if you knew your church were to be burned in one hour?" The sterling silver communion chalice? The brass candlesticks? Or today would it be the pastor's laptop?

Would we share the priorities of these three women, who carried the Hopefield Methodist Episcopal Bible to safety?

In the book of Jeremiah, the prophet is told by God to write down his words of warning to the people of Israel and Judah. The purpose of this written oracle was positive: "It may be that the house of Judah will hear all the evil which I purpose to do to them; that they may return every man from his evil way; that I may forgive their iniquity and their sin."[3]

But unlike the three women in the town of Hopefield, the king of Judah did not heed the warning of impending disaster.

As the warnings of Jeremiah were read aloud, ". . . the king cut it with the penknife, and cast it into the fire that was in the brazier, until all the scroll was consumed in the fire that was in the brazier."[4]

Do we value the Word of God? Does it challenge our lives enough to bring change, repentance and forgiveness? One thing is clear—the three women of Hopefield seemed to know that the Bible they saved had the message that could save them.

Lord, your Word is a light for my feet and a lamp for my path in a dark world. I pray that I might not only read the Word, but be transformed by it. Let me never take your Word for granted. Amen.

Notes

1. The Hopefield Bible is on display at the Crittenden County Museum in Earle, Arkansas. Photo taken by the author May 2016.
2. Reports on the attack on the steamer Hercules and burning of Hopefield, Ark., Feb. 17-19, 1863, U.S War Department, *The War of the Rebellion: A Compilation of the Official Records of the Union and Confederate Armies*, series 1, vol. 22, part I, 230-232; David O. Demuth, "The Burning of Hopefield," *Arkansas Historical Quarterly* 36, no. 2 (Summer 1977): 123-129.
3. Jeremiah 36:3 (World English Bible).
4. Jeremiah 36:23 (World English Bible).

This photo of two Confederate soldiers holding a Rebel battle flag at a Confederate reunion in 1917 is part of the Harris & Ewing Collection at the Library of Congress.[1]

15

Mixed Messages and Stained Symbols

First, I have to make a confession. I own a Confederate flag, more accurately known as the battle flag of the Army of Northern Virginia.

In my defense, I was ten years old when I received it. My older brother saw it in a store and said I needed it because it was part of my Southern heritage.

I didn't know much about my Confederate forbearers, although I was fascinated by the Civil War. Ironically, my sympathies were always more with the Yankees than the Rebels. I even asked for and received a blue Union uniform for Christmas when I was six years old. Still, I have kept the Rebel battle flag all these years. It's currently propped against a tall stack of Civil War books in my library.

But now that the Rebel flag has become a hot-button issue and Southern states are being hammered about getting rid of this symbol of the Confederacy, I'm far more ambivalent about it.

Are the stars and bars nothing more than an alternate symbol of the swastika? Are they symbols of slavery and racism? To some, yes. To the white supremacist who shot and killed the members of a Bible study at Emanuel African Methodist Episcopal Church in Charleston, South

Carolina, the flag is a rallying standard for hate. For the African-American, it may well be what the swastika is to the Jew—a symbol of oppression and genocide and brutality.

But there is another view. A view that makes me reluctant to burn my childhood battle flag or throw it in the trash. It symbolizes the schizophrenic inner conflict and the inner demons of our nation, and also the noblest, if misguided, aspiration for autonomy and sovereignty.

This is a conflict still not resolved.

The Black Lives Matter movement reminds us that there is still the feeling in the Black community that Black lives are regarded in our culture as subhuman, dispensable, and marginal.

And on the other hand, there are still those who argue that the Federal government overreaches its constitutional limits, and exceeds the rights that are reserved to the sovereign states.

And then there are those who have a stake in the south—who have ancestors who fought, bled, and died for the Confederacy, who have lived with the echoes of musket fire and the smell of cannon smoke. For them, there is a sense that this Rebel flag is more than a symbol of racism—although it is that. For them, it is more than a symbol of state's rights—although it is that. For them it is a symbol of valor and idealism—albeit misplaced and in the end defeated.

So for some of us, the Rebel flag creates a sense of ambivalence. Perhaps not unlike the brazen serpent that God told Moses to make in the wilderness of Sinai. The serpents had come among the Israelites and bitten them; and Moses told the Israelites to look at the brazen serpent and live.[2]

But some 500 years later, the serpent had become an object of worship, an idol. As part of his reforms, King Hezekiah took the dramatic step of destroying this relic from the past.[3]

This might be an argument on behalf of destroying the flags and removing them from public places in county seats and capitals.

Still, I haven't destroyed my flag. I haven't thrown it away. Not yet, anyway. It sits in the corner with my collection of facsimile minié balls and shelves of Civil War books.

The Rebel flag reminds me that even good, valorous, well-intentioned people can be absolutely <u>wrong</u> in their priorities and choices. And this might be an argument for allowing the flag to be displayed in museums, Confederate monuments, and Confederate cemeteries.

All of this debate provides a helpful dose of humility when I become too certain of my opinions and my ideologies.

Our Lord, give me a sense of clear discernment so that cultural symbols and historical artifacts don't become idols to me. Help me to focus my ultimate loyalties and allegiances only on you and your Kingdom. Amen.

Notes

1. *FLAGS. CONFEDERATE REUNION; BATTLE FLAGS OF WAR BETWEEN THE STATES* (Library of Congress, hec2008006132).
2. Numbers 21:4-9.
3. 2 Kings 18:1-4.

This photograph of the Elmira Cornet Band was taken June 1861 at Arlington, Virginia. A handwritten note on the border of this photo identifies the band as the *Band of the 8th New York State Militia*. However, based on information from the book, *Uncle Beebe, an American Civil War Narrative*, the staff at the Library of Congress have determined that the Elmira Cornet Band was a 16-piece regimental band who were part of the 33rd regiment of the New York State Volunteers. [1]

Soundtracks of the Civil War

Music certainly is the language of the soul. It gives expression to the deepest hopes and aches of the human heart. It emboldens and strengthens drooping arms.

Virtually every regiment had its own regimental band that typically played inspirational tunes before, during, and after the battles. The music that was played in the camps during those long hours and days between campaigns was extremely important to the morale of the ordinary soldier.

If we pay careful attention to the songs written and sung throughout the course of the war, we notice something very interesting. At the beginning of the war, the music was martial and full of bravado. The *Bonnie Blue Flag*, written in 1861, was second in popularity among Confederate soldiers only to *Dixie*. The chorus exulted:

> *Hurrah! Hurrah!*
> *For Southern rights hurrah!*
> *Hurrah for the Bonnie Blue Flag*
> *That bears a single star!* [2]

But as the war progressed and casualty rolls mounted, a melancholy tone began to appear. In 1863, Union troops sang around the campfire on the eve of battle:

Just before the battle, mother,
I am thinking most of you,
While upon the field we're watching
With the enemy in view.
Comrades brave are 'round me lying,
Filled with thoughts of home and God
For well they know that on the morrow,
Some will sleep beneath the sod. [3]

Like the Psalms in the Scriptures, the songs that were sung by these young men were an authentic cry of the heart, and reflected the many moods of these soldiers.

When I read the Psalms I can find a voice for any mood that I may experience—praise, grief, joy, anger. Through the Psalms, as with the therapy of music, I can work through some of my most intense experiences.

A few weeks after the one-sided and bloody battle of Fredericksburg in December 1862, Federal and Confederate forces were camped across the Rappahannock River from each other—approximately 100,000 Yankees and 70,000 Rebels.

Regimental bands on both sides played some favorite songs for their troops. It was a real "battle of the bands" as the Union and Confederate bands attempted to drown each other out.

And then something extraordinary happened. A Union band began to play a gentle melody that was instantly familiar to all the men on both sides of the river. Soon the Confederate bands joined in with the same tune.

The song struck a common chord with every man present that evening—*Home Sweet Home.*

Frank Mixson, a young South Carolina private, witnessed this "battle of the bands" that evening. He saw the extraordinary harmony that came together in that one song, expressing the heartfelt desire of every soldier, blue or gray:

There was not a sound from anywhere until the tune was finished . . . I
do believe that had we not had the river between us that the two armies
would have gone together and settled the war right there and then. [4]

Our Lord, when we sing the songs of our hearts, we are often the most open and the most vulnerable, and also the most energized and inspired. May we sing to you the true songs of our hearts. Amen.

Notes

1. *"Elmira Cornet Band," Thirty-third Regiment, of the New York State Volunteers, July 1861* (Library of Congress, 2013648631).
2. The tune of "The Bonnie Blue Flag" is a traditional Irish song, "The Irish Jaunting Car." There is a controversy about the authorship of the lyrics. It was published by Harry Macarthy as *The Bonnie Blue Flag,* (New Orleans, A.E. Blackmar &Bro., 1861). However, Gilberta S. Whittle attributes the lyrics to Mrs. Annie Chambers Ketchum in her article: "The Bonnie Blue Flag: Death of Mrs. Ketchum Recalls Her Stirring Southern War Song," *The Times-Dispatch* (Richmond, VA), January 31, 1904.
3. George F. Root, *Just Before the Battle, Mother*, (Chicago: Root & Cady, 1863).
4. Frank M. Mixson, *Reminiscences of a Private,* (Columbia: The State Company, 1910), 37-38

WAR AIN'T NO PICNIC

This aerial view of Fort Delaware was photographed by Michael Swanda, and recorded by the Philadelphia District of the U.S. Army Corps of Engineers. The Fort was built on Pea Patch Island, outside of Delaware City, Delaware. The documentation prepared by the U.S. Army Corps of Engineers provides this information:

Fort Delaware served as the primary defense of the Delaware River from the second quarter of the 19th century until the start of World War II. The Fort played an important role during the Civil War when the facility served as the largest prisoner of war camp in the North. A constant theme in the fort's history, represented by the sea wall, has been the need to exclude the tide from Pea Patch Island and to adequately drain the facilities thereon. Unsanitary conditions of the prisoner of war camp, in part stemming from poor drainage, gave the Fort the reputation of being the Union's counterpart to the infamous Confederate prisoner of war camp at Andersonville.[1]

17

Finding William

It began with vague family lore, and a weak hypothesis. Years ago my Grandpop told me a story about <u>his</u> grandad. It was short on detail, like a tale told to a child.

Grandpop said that my great-great grandfather had been a Rebel soldier from North Carolina during the Civil War. He was wounded and captured by the Yanks, and became a prisoner of war.

It seems he was in a prison near a river. Grandpop didn't know where the prison was. Wherever he was held, there was water flowing nearby. His buddies tried to persuade him to escape with them by swimming across, but he told them he couldn't because of his leg. That's all I knew of William Letchworth, my great-great grandfather.

My wife had been a little girl in Delaware City, Delaware in the early 1960's. She remembered that there was an island in the Delaware River that flowed past the city, called Pea Patch Island. She had heard that there had been a Civil War prison there once upon a time. But that's all she knew about it. A prison surrounded by water. Could William Letchworth have been there, I wondered?

It was a flimsy theory, but worth looking into, I thought. So, we visited her childhood home, and took the ferry across the Delaware

River to Pea Patch Island, where I was astonished to discover Fort Delaware, one of the best preserved pre-Civil War forts in the United States. Fort Delaware was, in fact, used as a Union prisoner of war camp.

I asked a living historian (who was dressed as a Union Captain) if there was a roster of Civil War prisoners. He led me to a computer monitor where I could search for William Letchworth. I was impressed to learn that there were more than 27,000 POW's who had passed through Fort Delaware the last year the war! Letchworth didn't appear on the list.

It had been a nice fantasy—that I would discover my roots in this old garrison on the Delaware River; that I would stand where my ancestor had gazed across the water yearning for freedom and home. Oh well.

But here was the surprise. A kind researcher heard of my inquiries. He had access to additional records of prisoners, and found that William D. Letchworth enlisted in the 44th North Carolina, company C on June 11, 1862. He was promoted to 5th sergeant sometime around February 1863. He was wounded at the Battle of Bristoe Station and was captured there on October 14, 1863. In June 1864, he was transferred to Fort Delaware, and remained there until he was paroled on a humanitarian prisoner exchange in September 1864!

I had stumbled upon the very tracks of my great-great grandfather! First, at Fort Delaware on Pea Patch Island. And then, based on this new information, my wife and I drove to Bristoe Station, Virginia. There I stood in the very field where William suffered a serious flesh wound in the right hip.

This search opened up layers and layers of information for me about my genealogy, going back to at least the 17th century. It was a gratifying experience.

However, I have also realized that I have a heritage that transcends genetics and family trees. Scripture tells me that because of my faith in Christ, I have an even deeper heritage that "takes after" my forbearer in the faith: "Even as Abraham 'believed God, and it was counted to him for righteousness.' Know therefore that those who are of faith, the same are children of Abraham."[2]

Not only that, but because of the redeeming work of Jesus Christ, we have the great privilege of being adopted as children of God: "And because you are children, God sent out the Spirit of his Son into your hearts, crying, 'Abba, Father!' So you are no longer a bondservant, but a son; and if a son, then an heir of God through Christ."[3]

If there is any "family tree" I want to be grafted into, it is the family of God!

Lord, I thank you for my human family. Although my family has faults, and even genetic liabilities, it is still the source of my origin. But even more, I thank you for adopting me into your family for the sake of my faith in Christ your Son. Amen.

Notes

1. *Fort Delaware, Pea Patch Island, Delaware City, New Castle County, DE* (Library of Congress, de0497). The full report can be accessed on the Library of Congress website:
   <http://cdn.loc.gov/master/pnp/habshaer/de/de0400/de0498/data/de0498data.pdf>
2. Galatians 3:6-7 (World English Bible).
3. Galatians 4:6-7 (World English Bible).

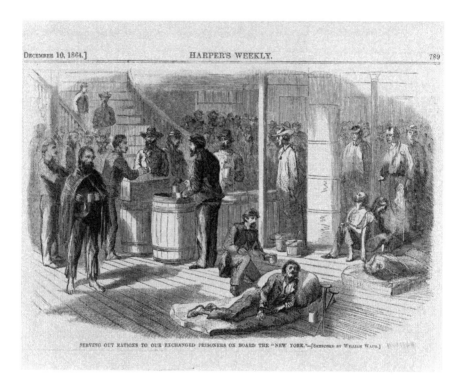

DECEMBER 10, 1864.]   HARPER'S WEEKLY.   789

SERVING OUT RATIONS TO OUR EXCHANGED PRISONERS ON BOARD THE "NEW YORK."—[SKETCHED BY WILLIAM WAUD.]

William Waud's sketch, *Serving out rations to our exchanged prisoners on board the "New York,"* appeared in the December 10, 1864 issue of *Harper's Weekly*. The *New York* was a vessel used for transporting paroled prisoners during the war.[1]

18

By His Wounds We Are Healed

From the top of the hill, one can look down across a field toward a fence, and beyond that a barn, and then about 150 yards beyond that—the railroad line. This was my perspective from the crest of the hill at the battlefield of Bristoe Station. Scarcely noted in most Civil War histories, it merits little more than a footnote.

Confederate General A. P. Hill was attempting to cut off a Union escape route, but as his Confederate troops advanced down the hill, they ran into determined, withering fire from Union artillery and rifles. All of this happened on an autumn afternoon—October 14, 1863. There were over 1400 Confederate casualties—killed, wounded, missing and captured. This was more than three times the casualties of the Federal forces. Later, when General Robert E. Lee viewed the aftermath of the battle with A. P. Hill, Lee reprimanded him and said, *Bury these poor men, and let us speak of it no more.*[2]

But I <u>must</u> speak of one of the casualties, one North Carolinian who was seriously wounded and captured by the Yankees. His name was William D. Letchworth, my great-great grandfather. He may have fought in some campaigns and skirmishes prior to this battle, without much incident.

WAR AIN'T NO PICNIC

On October 14, 1863, his luck ran out. William was a sergeant with Company C, 44th North Carolina Infantry Regiment. I can imagine him shouting orders and encouraging his men as they descended the hill toward the Union lines. But a severe flesh wound in his hip brought him down.

As the Confederate lines dissolved in disarray, the Union forces counterattacked and rushed up the hills, capturing many of the wounded Rebels who couldn't retreat with their comrades. William was one of those who was captured.

He spent the rest of the war in military hospitals and prisoner of war camps. William D. Letchworth was finally exchanged in a humanitarian parole in September 1864. His name vanishes from the military rolls for the rest of the war.

For my sake, his disappearance from Civil War history may have been a blessing. Had he not been wounded and captured, he might have fought at the Battle of the Wilderness, the Battle of Spotsylvania Court House, or the Siege of Petersburg.

That raises several questions. If William Letchworth had escaped unscathed and uncaptured at Bristoe Station, would he have been one of the many who died in the intense battles that followed? And if he had fallen, what would that have meant for my own existence? What would have become of Rosina Harris whom he married in 1867, who was to become the mother of Charles Henry, and the grandmother of Charles Walter, the great-grandmother of Clarence, and my own great-great grandmother?

It can be said that the wounds of William Letchworth might have insured my very existence!

Isaiah 53 reminds us of the wounds of Jesus. Isaiah writes: "But he was pierced for our transgressions. He was crushed for our iniquities. The punishment that brought our peace was on him; and by his wounds we are healed."[3]

My life may have been secured by the wounds sustained by William Letchworth. But all who trust in Christ can say: "By His wounds, we are healed."

Our Lord, I thank you for your willingness to be wounded for our sake, and to die that we might live. Amen.

Notes

1. William Waud, "Serving out rations to our exchanged prisoners on board the 'New York'" *Harper's Weekly* (December 10, 1864): 789; (also Library of Congress, 98501846).
2. Bill Backus and Robert Orrison, *A Want of Vigilance: The Bristoe Station Campaign, October 9-19, 1863* (El Dorado Hills: Savas Beatie, 2015), 89-96.
3. Isaiah 53:5.

One of the most unpopular Confederate generals, Braxton Bragg, was described by one of his staff members as having:

a peculiar conformation of eyebrows, which extended continuously from eye to eye, and a cold, steel-gray eye, which exhibited much of the white when animated, gave him in his sterner moods, or when roused, a very ferocious aspect, which made him a terror to all who incurred his displeasure.[1]

19

Braggin' Bragg

Seldom has there been such an opportunity to land a decisive blow in battle. General Braxton Bragg, commander of the Confederate Army of Tennessee, had been playing cat and mouse with General Rosecrans' Union corps. Bragg had evacuated Chattanooga, refusing to be trapped by Rosecrans. He didn't want Chattanooga to be a replay of the costly siege of Vicksburg.

Now Bragg had put together a brilliant strategy to lure Rosecrans to Chickamauga Creek. Rosecrans was so overconfident, he had split his army into three divisions, separated from one another by 15 to 20 miles. All Bragg had to do was hit them, one at a time, and he would have a decisive victory. It was within his grasp.[2]

He had one problem—Bragg was true to his name. He was autocratic, full of swagger and quarrelsome with his subordinates. It all boiled down to personality and leadership style.

Bragg was so quarrelsome, he even fought with himself! Prior to the outbreak of the Civil War, Bragg served as both a company commander and the company quartermaster in the U.S. Army. The quartermaster's job was to make sure that the flow of supplies and weapons to the troops continued steadily, and required a great deal of accountability.

His rigidity was legendary. Once, while he was temporarily in command of his company, he submitted a request for supplies to the quartermaster. Well, he himself was the quartermaster. And as the quartermaster, he denied the request! This absurdity continued awhile, with the request bouncing back and forth—to himself—until he finally brought the request to the Army post commander. The commander was flabbergasted: *My God, Mr. Bragg, you have quarreled with every officer in the army, and now you're quarrelling with yourself!*[3]

On September 19, 1863, the contentious General Bragg was poised at Chickamauga, ready to wipe out Rosecrans' Union army. However, he didn't receive unanimous cooperation from his staff officers. When he gave the order for his commanders to attack, some were at best lethargic; at worst, they were insubordinate. One of his generals, given the order to finish off a beleaguered Federal division at the break of dawn, was found on a farmhouse porch reading a paper and leisurely waiting for breakfast![4]

The Rebels won the battle of Chickamauga in September 1863. But because Bragg failed to contain and eradicate the Yankees, the Yanks escaped back to Chattanooga. There, the Union forces would soon receive a new commanding general—Ulysses S. Grant. Grant was no Rosecrans. He would not run away from a fight. Nor was he Bragg. Grant knew how to listen to and work with his subordinates.

General Nathan Bedford Forrest, who served under Bragg, was thoroughly disgusted by Bragg's failure to follow one blow with another. He confronted Bragg to his face and said: *You may as well not issue any more orders to me, for I will not obey them.... if you ever again try to interfere with me or cross my path it will be at the peril of your life.*[5]

It wasn't only his officers who found Bragg disagreeable. So did the enlisted men, whom he treated with harsh discipline. Private Sam Watkins, who fought in Bragg's army, wrote this:

None of General Bragg's soldiers ever loved him. They had no faith in his ability as a general. He was looked upon as a merciless tyrant. The soldiers were very scantily fed....He loved to crush the spirit of his men ....Not a single soldier in the whole army ever loved or respected him.[6]

Good leaders inspire. Good leaders care. Such qualities of leadership arouse confidence from those who follow. The apostle Peter tells the elders in the church: "Shepherd the flock of God which is among you, exercising the oversight, not under compulsion, but voluntarily, not for dishonest gain, but willingly; neither as lording it over those entrusted to you, but making yourselves examples to the flock."[7]

Our Lord, empower us to be positive, decisive leaders who know how to inspire loyalty in those who follow. And when we follow those who lead us, enable us to be team players who know how to listen and obey Godly instructions. Amen.

Notes

1. Colonel J. Stoddard Johnston is quoted by William Preston Johnston, *The Life of Gen. Albert Sidney Johnston* (New York: D. Appleton and Company, 1878) 547. The photo is titled *General Braxton Bragg* (Library of Congress, 2001695009).
2. David J. Eicher, *The Longest Night: A Military History of the Civil War* (New York: Simon & Schuster, 2001), 578.
3. Ulysses S. Grant, *Personal Memoirs of U.S. Grant, Vol. 2* (New York: Charles L. Webster & Company, 1886), 86-87.
4. The general was Leonidas Polk. Thomas Lawrence Connelly, *Autumn of Glory: The Army of Tennessee, 1862-1865* (Baton Rouge: Louisiana State University Press, 1971), 216-217.
5. Dr. J.B. Cowan was present when Forrest confronted Bragg and personally relayed the conversation to Wyeth. John Allan Wyeth, *Life of General Nathan Bedford Forrest* (New York: Harper & Brothers Publishers, 1899) 265-266.
6. Sam R. Watkins, *"Co. Aytch," Maury Grays, First Tennessee Regiment*, 2nd ed. (Chattanooga: The Chattanooga Times, 1900), 39.
7. Hebrews 13:17 (World English Bible).

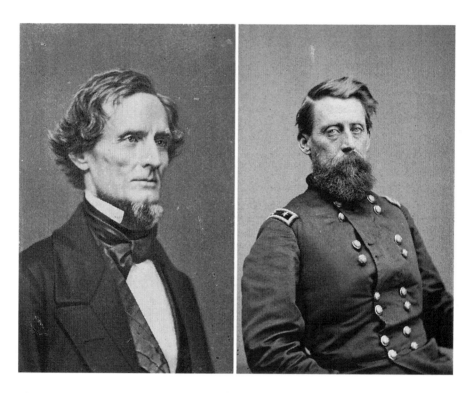

These two men had only one thing in common—they were both named *Jefferson Davis*. They couldn't be more different. The Jefferson Davis on the left, Jefferson Finis Davis, was the first and only president of the Confederate States of America. The "other Jeff Davis" was Union General Jefferson Columbus Davis.[1,2]

Jeff Davis Doppelganger

Sometimes a case of mistaken identity can be extremely dangerous. There were two men during the Civil War who shared the same famous name. Jefferson Davis.

One was the first—and last—president of the Confederate States of America. He was a wealthy plantation owner from Mississippi who had also served the United States prior to the Civil War as a U.S. congressman and senator, and the 23rd United States Secretary of War. He had also served in the Mexican American War as the colonel of a volunteer regiment. And he was a stalwart defender of slavery.

The second Jefferson Davis was also a veteran of the Mexican American War. He was born in Memphis—Indiana! The significant difference between the two men is that this Jeff Davis was an officer in the Union Army. He was one of the officers at Fort Sumter when the first artillery salvo of the war began. He distinguished himself at the battle of Pea Ridge, and was rewarded with a promotion to Brigadier General.

Obviously, two very different men, right? The Jeff Davis who served as the president of the Confederacy in Richmond, Virginia; and Jeff Davis the Union officer. There was never any confusion of identity, right?

Well, there was one occasion.

WAR AIN'T NO PICNIC

During the Battle of Chickamauga in September 1863, night fell on the soldiers of the 21st Ohio. They were expecting Union reinforcements. When a regiment of soldiers came over the Horseshoe Ridge, it was impossible to tell in that twilight whether they wore Union blue or Rebel butternut.

One of the Union soldiers, standing as a picket, called out, *What troops are you?* The approaching soldiers hollered back, *Jeff Davis' troops!* Naturally, the Union soldiers assumed that they were the troops of the Union General Jeff Davis, who was commanding two brigades of the 20th Ohio division. At last, they thought, reinforcements from their own Ohio had arrived!

The Union soldiers relaxed as they welcomed the newcomers to their lines, but moments later, the fixed-bayonet muzzles of the 7th Florida Confederates were leveled at their heads! These troops were loyal to the *other* Jeff Davis—the Confederate president. The vulnerable Ohioans had to surrender.[3]

There is another very famous instance of two people who share the same name that is found in the Bible.

Jesus of Nazareth was given his name even before he was born. In Luke's Gospel, the Angel Gabriel appears to Mary and tells her: "You will conceive in your womb, and give birth to a son, and will call his name 'Jesus.'"[4] The name Jesus is a Greek version of the Hebrew name *Joshua*, which means *the Lord Saves.* Obviously, this is true of Jesus of Nazareth who was crucified and who rose from the dead. Our faith in his life, death and resurrection secures our salvation.

But there was another man named *Jesus* in the New Testament. When Jesus of Nazareth was on trial for his life before Pontius Pilate, Barabbas was also in Roman custody. According to some ancient authorities, Barabbas' full name was actually *Jesus Barabbas*. Pilate offered the people of Jerusalem a choice—he would free either Jesus of Nazareth, or Jesus Barabbas.[5]

Like the two Jefferson Davises, these two men couldn't have been more different. The one Jesus was virgin-born, the Son of God, the Savior of the World, who died that we might be freed from sin, whose love overcomes hate, and whose resurrection overcomes death. The second Jesus can best be described as a bandit or a terrorist. He is described as one of the rebels who had committed murder during the insurrection.[6] This may mean that Jesus Barabbas was a member of the Zealots, a violent faction in Palestine which sought the overthrow of imperial Roman power.

This raises the inevitable question for us—are we inclined to follow the Jesus who is the Prince of Peace, or the Jesus who represents the values that perpetuate violence and hatred in our world? Do we know Jesus of Nazareth well enough to recognize him, even when times are dark?

Our Lord, the choices are clear. There is a way of love that draws us closer to you; and there is a way of hate that takes us away from you. When we name the name of Jesus, may we be sure that we are following the Jesus of Light and Life, not darkness and death. Amen.

Notes

1. Jefferson Davis (Library of Congress, No. brh2003002998/PP)
2. Maj. Gen. Jefferson C. Davis
   (Library of Congress, No. cwp2003003808/PP)
3. Silas S. Canfield, History of the 21st Regiment Ohio Volunteer Infantry in the War of the Rebellion (Toledo: Vrooman, Anderson & Bateman, Printers, 1893), 148; Captains Vantine and Gillespie gave a similar report on September 27, 1863, U.S War Department, The War of the Rebellion: A Compilation of the Official Records of the Union and Confederate Armies, series 1, vol. 30, part I, 395.
4. Luke 1:31 (World English Bible).
5. See Matthew 27:15-17 in the New International Version or the New Revised Standard Version.
6. Mark 15:7.

By telegraph from Fort Monroe

Head-Quarters Military Division of the Mississippi,

In the Field 186

Savannah, Dec 22 1864

To his Excellency,
President Lincoln,

I beg to present you as a Christmas Gift the City of Savannah, with one hundred and fifty (150) heavy guns and plenty of ammunition, and also about twenty five thousand (25000) bales of cotton

W. T. Sherman
Maj Genl.

Major General William Tecumseh Sherman sent this telegram to President Abraham Lincoln, informing him that not only had he captured Savannah, but he had spared it as well.[1]

21

The Christmas Gift

It was a unique Christmas present. On December 22, 1864, Major General William T. Sherman completed a six-week "scorched earth" march through Georgia, from Atlanta to the port city of Savannah.

Even today, many Georgians despise the name of Sherman as the man who "drove old Dixie down." For many Southerners, Sherman's name is synonymous with Hitler.

General Sherman's rationale for these devastating tactics was based on his philosophy that the more war he brought to the heartland of Georgia, the better it would be for all in the long run: *War is cruelty. There is no use trying to reform it. The crueler it is, the sooner it will be over.*[2]

And yet, this ruthless general, who is still excoriated in the South, exhibited both a sense of humor and a quality of mercy.

After the surrender of Savannah, Sherman dispatched a telegram to President Lincoln in Washington D.C. with the message: *I beg to present you, as a Christmas gift, the city of Savannah, with 150 heavy guns and plenty of ammunition, and also about 25,000 bales of cotton.*[3]

As one who has visited my grandparents in Savannah, I'm happy to reflect on the more merciful side of Sherman's character. Although

Sherman's troops burned and looted their way three hundred miles from Atlanta to the coast, he ordered that the city of Savannah be spared.

There are several theories offered to explain Sherman's mercy. One theory is that he was persuaded by a lovely Southern belle to have compassion on her hometown. Another theory is that it was the Christmas season, and he was filled with Christmas cheer. Another is more practical—that he needed to keep the port of Savannah intact for strategic military purposes.

What ultimately matters to me is that this beautiful city, with the antebellum homes and the Spanish moss, still stands. Perhaps, in addition to the military and political considerations, Sherman simply saw that this was a beautiful city, and it softened his hard heart.

In the Book of Exodus, we find another "scorched earth" battle waged on a cosmic level. Through Moses, God wreaks havoc on the economic and religious life of Pharaoh and the people of Egypt. God's objective is to persuade Pharaoh to let God's people go free.

Unfortunately, Pharaoh's heart was hardened by his own resistance, and then God gave him over to his hard heart: ". . . he hardened his heart, and didn't listen to them, as Yahweh had spoken."[4]

However we may understand the mercy of Sherman, which led to Savannah's preservation; or the hard-heartedness of the Pharaoh, which led to the plagues of Egypt and the liberation of Israel, we do well to heed the appeal of scripture in our own lives: "Today if you will hear his voice, don't harden your hearts, as in the rebellion."[5]

Lord, soften our hearts so that we may hear and heed your Word. And as we have received mercy from you, may we extend mercy to others. Amen.

Notes

1. *Telegram from General William T. Sherman to President Abraham Lincoln announcing the surrender of Savannah, Georgia, as a Christmas present to the President.* (National Archives, No. 301637) This is part of the National Archives Series: *Telegrams Sent by the Field Office of the Military Telegraph and Collected by the Office of the Secretary of Ar., 1860-1870.*
2. Grenville M. Dodge, *Personal Recollections of President Abraham Lincoln, General Ulysses S. Grant, and General William T. Sherman* (Council Bluffs: The Monarch Printing Company, 1914), 142.
3. The Abraham Lincoln Papers at the Library of Congress: *Series 1. General Correspondence. 1833-1916. William T. Sherman to Abraham Lincoln, Thursday, December 22, 1864 (Telegram offering Savannah, Georgia as a Christmas present)* (Library of Congress).
4. Exodus 8:15 (World English Bible).
5. Hebrews 3:15 (World English Bible) The author of Hebrews is quoting Psalm 95:7b-8 "Today, oh that you would hear his voice! Don't harden your heart, as at Meribah, as in the day of Massah in the wilderness. . ."

George N. Barnard photographed this soldier pretending to light a Quaker gun with his linstock. Used to deceive the enemy, Quaker guns were logs painted to look like cannons. Aptly named, since the Quakers were pacifists who believed in non-violence.[1]

Numbers Aren't Everything

Sheer numbers can turn the tide in battle. In most of the battles of the Civil War, the North possessed a decisive numerical advantage over the secessionist South.

In 1863, at the peak of enlistment for both sides, the Union armies outnumbered the Confederates by a more than 2 to 1 margin.

And yet in so many cases, Northern generals were outmaneuvered, out-strategized, and outsmarted by Southern generals. Numbers were not always the determining factor.

At Yorktown, Virginia, March 8-9, 1862, Confederate General Jeb Magruder held off the Union Army of the Potomac, commanded by General George McClellan. Magruder commanded only 11,000 troops, compared to McClellan's 121,500.

Despite the odds, Magruder was able to paralyze McClellan by marching the same troops around and around in a circle, and from camp to camp along the line, giving the impression that the Rebels had far more troops than they did.

Magruder topped off this performance by initiating a massive artillery barrage against the Army of the Potomac. And when the shelling suddenly stopped and the battlefield grew quiet, the Union troops cautiously crept toward the Confederate guns -- only to discover that the Confederate army and their actual guns were gone! What they found were logs painted black to resemble cannons. They had been menaced by what came to be called "Quaker Guns" because even pacifists could have no objection to cannons that posed no danger to anyone.

A mere 11,000 soldiers were able to stymie 121,500 by applying tactical theatrics.

The Scriptures also teach us that numbers aren't everything.

In the book of Judges, we are reminded of Gideon. He was preparing for battle against Midian with good numbers—23,000 Israelites. But the Lord began to whittle away at those numbers. He told Gideon to send home those who were afraid, and reduced the army to 10,000. And then God directed Gideon to reduce that army down to 300.

Those 300 went into battle against Midian and won a terrific victory! With 300 men, Gideon encircled the Midianites and Amalekites, whose soldiers were encamped in a valley. Their armies were described to be as massive as an infestation of locusts, "and their camels were without number, as the sand on the seashore."[2]

Gideon equipped his men with torches inside clay jars, and trumpets. At a synchronized signal, in the darkness of night when the guards in the camp were changing their shift, the 300 Israelites broke their clay jars, blew their trumpets and shouted: "The sword of the Lord and of Gideon!"[3]

The Midianites and the Amalekites were so disoriented, they turned their swords on one another, and Gideon's small forces prevailed without much effort!

David knew what it was to be consistently outnumbered. And yet he consistently triumphed over his enemies. Goliath was massive, and David small and young, yet David prevailed. And David writes in the Psalms that the presence of the Lord more than compensates when he is outnumbered: "Though an army should encamp against me, my heart shall not fear; Though war should rise against me, even then I will be confident."[4]

Numbers Aren't Everything

God isn't interested in numbers for their own sake. Jesus was able to turn the world upside down with just twelve ordinary men. We need not be discouraged when we see only a few who are on God's side. God can work wonders with a handful of people.

Our Lord, we know that you are not impressed by numbers, like we are. When only a handful of people are truly surrendered to you, they can do far more than a massive number who are lukewarm. Use the few to challenge the many. Amen.

Notes

1. G.N. Barnard photographed *Centreville, Virginia. Quaker gun.* Originally a stereograph, this is the right plate. The caption from the negative sleeve reads: *Quaker Guns, Centreville, March 1862.* (Library of Congress, cwp2003005042/PP).
2. Judges 7:12 (World English Bible).
3. Judges 7:20 (King James Version).
4. Psalm 27:3 (World English Bible).

Lula McLean's doll is on exhibit at the Appomattox Court House National Historical Park. The doll was in the McLean's parlor when Generals Lee and Grant met there to negotiate Lee's surrender. Lt. Col. Thomas Moore took the doll as a war souvenir, giving it the nickname, *The Silent Witness.*[1]

Coming Full Circle

Some people say that the Civil War started in Wilmer McLean's front yard and ended in his parlor. McLean's home was situated on the family estate in Prince William County, Virginia, near a stream called *Bull Run*. General P. G. T. Beauregard saw this as a perfect location for setting up Confederate headquarters during the Battle of Blackburn's Ford. (This was a preliminary skirmish to the first major land battle of the Civil War—*The First Battle of Bull Run*, also known as the *Battle of First Manassas*.)

On July 18, 1861, General Beauregard and his staff were anticipating dinner at the McLean home when a Federal cannonball crashed through the kitchen. Beauregard's chief signal officer recalled:

> *. . . our dinner was ruined by the mud daubing between the logs jarred out as the shell passed through both walls falling into the sliced up meat & dished up vegetables, and we went without dinner that day.*[2]

The McLean family had been living peacefully on what they called "Yorkshire Plantation" since 1854. But now the peace was broken. Now the war had invaded their front yard.

Wilmer McLean moved his family far away from the movement of troops. As he later told General Alexander: *My whole plantation was ruined and I sold out and came way off here over 200 miles to this out of the way place where I hoped I never would see another soldier of either side*.[3] They moved to a small, obscure town south of Bull Run—Appomattox Court House, Virginia. As the war progressed, McLean worked as a sugar broker for the Confederacy and was able to keep his household away from the guns of war . . . until April 9, 1865.

General Ulysses S. Grant, commanding the Union Army of the Potomac, had pursued and cornered General Robert E. Lee's army—not far from Appomattox Court House. Lee saw that his soldiers were willing, but simply no longer capable of resisting the overwhelming numbers and resources of the Union Army. General Lee communicated to General Grant that he was ready to surrender.

Lee dispatched an officer to procure a room where he and General Grant could meet face-to-face. The officer found a suitable two-story house in town. The house, of course, was Wilmer McLean's home!

General Robert E. Lee entered the McLean house in his best dress uniform, brass, braid and all. A little later, General Grant rode up on his horse, still wearing his rumpled, muddy field uniform. The two generals negotiated the terms for the surrender in Wilmer McLean's parlor.

It was a historic moment—and the Union officers were very aware of that. Once the surrender had been negotiated and Lee had returned to his troops, the officers began stripping the house. The desk, pen, chairs, and even Lula McLean's doll became "souvenirs." In their defense, they did thrust money into McLean's hands, but over McLean's strenuous objections.[4]

Wilmer McLean almost literally saw the Civil War from beginning to end. How many of us get to see the beginning and the end of all of our enterprises?

We have One who sees all time and all history in their entirety, from beginning to end. In fact that is what he calls himself: "Behold, I come quickly. My reward is with me, to repay to each man according to his work. I am the Alpha and the Omega, the First and the Last, the Beginning and the End."[5]

Christ, the true beginning and the end, is the ultimate peacemaker. In his house, all war shall cease.

Our Lord, you are our true beginning and our ultimate end—our fulfillment. Please finish what you have started in our lives, and bring us to completion in Christ. Amen.

Notes

1. Joe Williams and Ryan Henry, "Lula McLean's Rag Doll" *National Park Service U.S. Department of the Interior.*
   < https://www.nps.gov/apco/kids-rag-doll.htm> (Photo courtesy of Appomattox Court House National Historical Park.)
2. Gary W. Gallagher, ed., *Fighting for the Confederacy: The Personal Recollections of General Edward Porter Alexander* (Chapel Hill: The University of North Carolina Press, 1989), 46.
3. Ibid., 48.
4. Horace Porter, *Campaigning with Grant* (New York: The Century Co., 1906), 466-488.
5. Revelation 22:12-13 (World English Bible).

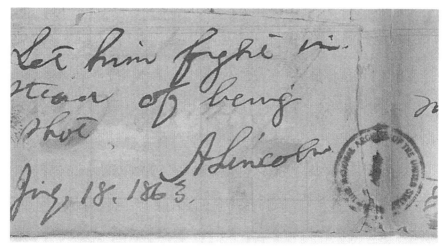

Michael Delaney, a Colorado army private, deserted his regiment, then re-enlisted with a different regiment months later, using a different name. After being discovered, he was court martialed for desertion and sentenced to be executed. On July 18, 1863, President Abraham Lincoln read over the private's case and wrote these words at the bottom of an official document:

Let him fight instead of being shot.[1]

24

Pardon Me

As the Civil War progressed, it became inevitable that some Union soldiers would face military justice for one reason or another. Some charges were deadly serious, such as desertion or cowardice in battle. Sometimes the dereliction could be potentially dangerous to their own troops, like the sentry who simply fell asleep, or worse, abandoned his post.

Military justice was stern. Beyond floggings, the swiftest retribution was execution by firing squad.

But Abraham Lincoln had a deep compassionate streak. If he could be gotten to by an interceding wife, a mother, or aging father—he was more than likely inclined to sign a pardon.

One thing Lincoln hated was the routine sound of rifle fire that could be heard echoing from across the Potomac River on Fridays. He confessed to an Army chaplain: *This is the day when they shoot deserters. I am wondering whether I have used the pardoning power as much as I ought.*[2]

When he himself was shot, none mourned more than those who had been the beneficiaries of Lincoln's mercy. Sergeant Smith Stimmel, one of the members of Lincoln's bodyguard detail, wrote an invaluable memoir of his experiences with President Lincoln. He describes an encounter that one of his fellow troopers had the day after the assassination:

During that day one of my comrades . . . was riding down street, and he met another cavalryman from another troop, a man he did not know, and the fellow was weeping. They stopped and had a passing word about the sad event of the night before, and, speaking of the President's death, the stranger said to my comrade, "It probably means more to me than it does to you; he signed an order that saved me from being shot."[3]

Stimmel offers his interpretation of this conversation:

When we recount how he saved many from being shot, I often think how the words that were applied to our Savior as he hung upon the cross, might be applied to Lincoln, though in a different sense: "He saved others; himself he cannot save."[4]

It doesn't escape notice that Lincoln was shot on Good Friday. But there is, of course, a significant difference between Lincoln and Jesus.

Many years ago, I heard the Reverend Dr. Robert E. Lee Bearden deliver a sermon about the atoning death of Jesus. He pointed out the unintended irony of the scornful mockers as Jesus was dying:

"Those who passed by blasphemed him, wagging their heads, and saying, 'You who destroy the temple, and build it in three days, save yourself! If you are the Son of God, come down from the cross!' Likewise the chief priests also mocking, with the scribes, the Pharisees, and the elders, said, 'He saved others, but he can't save himself. If he is the King of Israel, let him come down from the cross now, and we will believe in him.'"[5]

Dr. Bearden, in his gentle and eloquent manner, made it clear that by <u>not</u> saving himself, Jesus saves us. He could not save himself <u>and</u> save us as well. His death was necessary in order for us to live.

Our Lord, we thank you that you were willing to pay the ultimate price for our salvation, knowing that you could not save us without your own death. And we are even more grateful knowing that death itself could not hold you in the grave. Amen.

Notes

1. John Ingold, "The Seven Famous Words that Spared a Colorado Soldier 150 Years Ago" *The Denver Post*, July 18, 2013.
   Mr. Ingold cropped the image, which was used courtesy of the National Archives. He granted permission to use this cropped image and the information in his article.
   < http://blogs.denverpost.com/crime/2013/07/18/the-seven-famous-words-that-spared-a-colorado-soldier-150-years-ago/5096/>
2. John Eaton, *Grant, Lincoln and the Freedmen: Reminiscences of the Civil War* (New York: Longmans, Green, and Co., 1907), 180.
3. Smith Stimmel, *Personal Reminiscences of Abraham Lincoln* (Minneapolis: William H.M. Adams, 1928), 89.
4. Ibid.
5. Matthew 27:39-42 (World English Bible).

This photo was taken by Thomas W. Bankes on April 26, 1865 while the *Sultana* was docked in Helena, Arkansas, less than twenty-four hours before the disaster.[1] The number of passengers exceeded the ship's legal capacity by over six times. Survivor A.C. Brown remembers discussing the crowded conditions with the ship's clerk. When Sgt. Brown asked how many were on board:

> *The clerk replied that if we arrived safe at Cairo it would be the greatest trip ever made on the western waters, as there were more people on board than were ever carried on one boat on the Mississippi River.*[2]

25

Do Your Job!

It was a catastrophe and a scandal. Over 1,800 lives were lost when the steamboat *Sultana* exploded and sank in the Mississippi River on April 27, 1865. But it was more than just a catastrophe. The *Sultana* disaster exposed the ugly, grubby underbelly of greed and graft during the Civil War.

From the *Sultana*'s captain, to its ship engineer—this is a story of sordid self-interest and dereliction of duty.

It wasn't just the ship's captain and the engineer who were corrupt. At the top of this sleazy pyramid was Lt. Col. Reuben Hatch. In 1861, he was implicated for receiving bribes as assistant regimental quartermaster in Cairo, Illinois, but because of political connections he had not been convicted.[3]

By April 1865, Hatch had "flopped to the top" and was the chief quartermaster for the Union Department of the Mississippi.[4] One of his duties was arranging transportation for newly-released Union soldiers from the Confederate prison camps to their homes in the north. The quartermaster's office was authorized to book passage for them on civilian steamboats.

WAR AIN'T NO PICNIC

The Federal Government was willing to pay transportation costs for these prisoners of war—$5 for enlisted men and $10 for officers. Hatch colluded with other officers who were just as greedy as he was. They could profit from these poor prisoners of war.[5]

The level of corruption was so tangled, it is almost impossible to unravel. Hatch and his officers were in collusion with Captain Mason of the *Sultana*, and they had every financial incentive to pack as many bodies aboard the steamboat as they could. So overbooked was the boat that most of these frail, emaciated soldiers couldn't find a place to sit or lie down.[6] Corporal George M. Clinger remembers: *We were driven on like so many hogs until every foot of standing room was occupied.*[7]

And there was another layer of culpability. Captain Mason, the skipper of the *Sultana*, was made aware by the chief engineer, Nathan Wintringer, that the boilers were spent and required massive repairs. Wintringer enlisted the help of a boilermaker in Vicksburg named R.G. Taylor to address the problem.

Taylor's inspection revealed a dangerous bulge on the middle boiler which would require several days to repair. But Captain Mason was in a hurry. He needed the revenue this trip would bring—fast. Wintringer pleaded with a reluctant Taylor to make temporary repairs so they could get under way. He assured Taylor that he would make sure the proper repairs would be made when they arrived upriver—at St. Louis. (Unfortunately, the *Sultana* never made it to St. Louis.)

Taylor at first refused to make any repairs unless he were permitted to do the right thing. He finally gave in and grudgingly did the bare patchwork necessary to get the *Sultana* back on the river.[8]

What makes the sinking of the *Sultana* so catastrophic is the sheer number of lives lost. It is the largest maritime disaster in American history. Although the estimates may be even higher, at least 1,800 perished in the disaster. What made it so tragic was the cruel irony that these men were full of hope and anticipation. After enduring years of war and surviving the abysmal conditions of Andersonville and Catawba (two of the most notorious prison camps in the war), they were finally going home.

From the captain to the quartermaster and his staff, there was a systematic pattern of corruption and greed. "He who is greedy for gain troubles his own house, but he who hates bribes will live."[9]

The engineer and the boilermaker were also complicit in their negligence and irresponsibility. The engineer knew better. The boilermaker caved under pressure.

We are reminded that our work matters, and that such things as responsibility, diligence, and safety do make a difference. "Whatever you do, work heartily, as for the Lord, and not for men, knowing that from the Lord you will receive the reward of the inheritance; for you serve the Lord Christ."[10]

Our Lord, remind us that our work matters. Inspire us, whether we are accountants, nurses, sales representatives, or, yes, boilermakers, to do our work with integrity; motivated not by greed, but for your glory. Amen.

Notes

1. *Helena, Arkansas. April 26, 1865. Ill-fated Sultana* (Library of Congress, 2013647457).
2. Chester D. Berry, *Loss of the Sultana and Reminiscences of Survivors* (Lansing: Darius D. Thorp, Printer and Binder, 1892), 77-78.
3. Jerry O. Potter, *The Sultana Tragedy: America's Greatest Maritime Disaster* (Gretna: Pelican Publishing Company, 1992), 32-33.
4. Ibid., 32.
5. Berry, 47-48.
6. The legal capacity of the *Sultana* was 376 passengers plus 85 crewmembers. Estimates are that the *Sultana* was carrying up to 2,500 people on that tragic voyage! Potter, 5 & 70.
7. Berry, 97.
8. Potter, 51.
9. Proverbs 15:27 (World English Bible).
10. Colossians 3:23-24 (World English Bible).

EXPLOSION OF THE STEAMER "SULTANA," April 28, 1865.

Harper's Weekly published this drawing in their May 20, 1865 issue.[1]
The date in the caption is incorrect (April 28, 1865). The explosion of the
Sultana occurred at about 2 a.m. on April 27.

The Sultana Angel

It was a nightmarish scenario—an overcrowded steam boat chugging up the Mississippi River in the chill darkness of an April morning. Rocking from the excess weight, the *Sultana* seemed to stagger like a drunk, as it moved upriver. With each tilt of the deck, the water in the ship's boilers sloshed back and forth, creating hot spots, building to an impossible level of pressure. At 2:00 a.m. on April 27, 1865, three of the *Sultana*'s four boilers exploded with a huge flash of fire, smoke and scalding steam.[2]

> *What a crash! My God! My blood curdles while I write and words are*
> *inadequate…. Such hissing of steam, the crash of the different decks….*
> *The falling of the massive smoke stacks, the death cry of strong-*
> *hearted men caught in every conceivable manner, the red-tongued*
> *flames bursting up through the mass of humanity….* [3]

The passengers and crew were faced with the stark choice of fire or water. Only in the deadly currents of the river was there any hope at all. By the hundreds they plunged into the cold, swift waters of the Mississippi, fleeing the flames. Of the 2,400 aboard the *Sultana*, only 600 survived that horrific night.[4]

Notable among the civilians was a handful of women from the Ladies Christian Commission. This organization provided religious literature, Bibles, medical assistance and spiritual consolation to Union soldiers throughout the war.

A member of the Ladies Christian Commission watched in horror as the survivors in the water forgot themselves, fighting as drowning people will do for every breath, dragging down those who were around them into waters of death. She exhorted the men to remember themselves, to remember their humanity, and to spare their comrades. According to a survivor, Chester Berry, her pleas calmed the frantic men:

> One of these ladies, with more than ordinary courage, when the flames at last drove all the men from the boat, seeing them fighting like demons in the water in the mad endeavor to save their lives, actually destroying each other and themselves by their wild actions, talked to them, urging them to be men, and finally succeeded in getting them quieted down ...

Having regained at least a measure of composure, those in the river became concerned about this woman on the burning deck. They saw her silhouette against the demonic brilliance of the flames. They screamed for her to jump into the water, and save herself.

She hesitated. Their heads were bobbing so close to one another, she saw that she would only harm them if she jumped into the water.

> And so, rather than run the risk of becoming the cause of the death of a single person, she folded her arms quietly over her bosom and burned, a voluntary martyr to the men she had so lately quieted. [5]

In the words of her Savior Jesus Christ: "Greater love has no one than this, that someone lay down his life for his friends."[6] Jesus is the supreme example of sacrificial love, and the source of our atonement through his own death for our salvation.

We are called as followers of Jesus to imitate his sacrificial love. Not many of us are offered the extreme opportunity to sacrifice our lives as this woman on the *Sultana* did. But all of us can serve others through missions, service, and simple compassion.

Our Lord, sacrificial love is at the heart of your cross; we pray that we may follow your example and offer ourselves for others as a living sacrifice. Amen.

Notes

1. *Explosion of the steamer SULTANA, April 28, 1865* (Library of Congress, 2002699583).
2. Alan Huffman, *Sultana* (New York: Harper, 2009), 191, 244.
3. Chester D. Berry, *Loss of the Sultana and Reminiscences of Survivors* (Lansing: Darius D. Thorp, Printer and Binder, 1892), 191-192.
4. Exact numbers are nearly impossible to calculate, but incomplete records give us an idea of the passenger and crew manifest: 85 crewmembers, 100 civilians, and 2,317 Union soldiers recently released from Confederate prison camps. Jerry O. Potter, *The Sultana Tragedy: America's Greatest Maritime Disaster* (Gretna: Pelican Publishing Company, 1992), 195-196.
5. Berry, 10.
6. John 15:13 (World English Bible).

Franklin Hardin Barton was one of the Arkansans who endeavored to rescue the victims of the *Sultana* disaster. In all likelihood, he is the mysterious Confederate rescuer in Union Captain J. Walter Elliott's report. Elliott describes an anonymous Confederate soldier who disappeared after making sure those he had rescued were safely on board the *Jenny Lind* steamer:

> But what had become of my chivalrous knight of the gray? How he dignified "the gray." Silently he had disappeared when his good work was done, with that modesty inseparable from true royalty of heart. Would that I knew his name.[1]

The Rescuers

The explosion on the Mississippi River could be heard for miles. The fire on the sinking hulk lit the night sky. When the *Sultana* steamboat exploded on that dark, nightmarish morning of April 27, 1865, nearly 1,800 of the 2,400 passengers drowned or were burned to death.

These passengers were primarily Union soldiers recently released from the notorious Confederate Andersonville and Cahaba prison camps. But some of the rescuers who responded to the disaster were Arkansans, whose sympathies inclined toward the Confederacy. In fact, one of the rescuers was wearing the gray uniform jacket he had worn as a Confederate soldier.

But these citizens of Mound City, Arkansas could see the burning *Sultana* blazing on the river as they stood on the banks of the Mississippi. They <u>had</u> to do something!

Ironically, most of them were limited because they had no boats. (During the war, Union soldiers smashed the hulls of boats that these southerners owned on the pretext that Confederate guerrillas might use the boats to carry out acts of war and sabotage against Union forces.) So, they lashed logs together with rope and pushed themselves out into the swift current toward the steamboat.

The water was chilling, below 60 degrees, lowering the body heat of those who had leapt into the river. Swimming against the powerful Mississippi current would be physically exhausting for a normal man— but these were men whose strength had been sapped by horrible conditions in the prison camps.

The scene must have been horrific for the rescuers—hundreds of living and dead bodies floated in the water as the morning dawned. Some survivors clung desperately to the sinking hull. Victims shrieked and moaned from scalding burns and freezing water.

Anyone who has ever been trained as a lifeguard understands the dangers of rescuing a drowning victim. All rationality is gone. The victim's instinct is to find something, anything, to which they might cling. Panic ensues, putting even the rescuer at risk when the victim claws and scratches for life, trying to stay afloat.

The rescuers had to be cautious. There were so many in the water and on the burning hull of the steamboat that an attempt to pull all of them out at once would result in a swamped raft—and then rescuers and victims would all be in peril!

One of the survivors, Corporal Fast, stood on the burning deck of the *Sultana* and watched as an Arkansas farmer named John Fogleman poled out on a makeshift raft toward the steamboat. Fast describes the scene:

> About eight o'clock we saw a man put off from the Arkansas shore with two hewn logs lashed together ... He came within about six rods of us and our burning boat, and then stopped for a parley. He said that he could carry only six of us, and if more got on we would all drown. He was afraid to come nearer lest all should leap overboard and get on to his logs.[2]

They agreed that Fogleman would take six at a time, and then return. He did so again and again. Even after the hull sank, steaming and hissing into the river, he returned to the partially submerged trees near the shore to rescue those clinging to their branches.[3]

To be approached by men on a raft must have seemed like salvation to the desperate survivors. All of us are in peril. We all share the moral peril of sin. And we desperately need the rescue that only Christ can provide.

The Apostle Paul actually knew the experience of shipwreck, and he describes salvation from the perspective of one who desperately needs to be rescued: "we felt that we had received the sentence of death so that we would rely not on ourselves but on God who raises the dead. He who rescued us from so deadly a peril will continue to rescue us; on him we have set our hope that he will rescue us again."[4]

Christ is our ultimate rescuer, who pushes out into the nightmare of our shipwreck and brings us safely to shore.

Our Lord, we give you thanks for the ultimate Rescuer, who not only has risked his life but has given his life that he might draw us to safety. Thank you for rescuing us from sin and death. Amen.

Notes

1. Chester D. Berry, *Loss of the Sultana and Reminiscences of Survivors* (Lansing: Darius D. Thorp, Printer and Binder, 1892), 122.
   Photo courtesy of Judge John N. Fogleman, a descendant of Franklin Hardin Barton.
2. Jesse Hawes, *Cahaba: A Story of Captive Boys in Blue* (New York: Burr Printing House, 1888), 172-174.
3. Jerry O. Potter, *The Sultana Tragedy: America's Greatest Maritime Disaster* (Gretna: Pelican Publishing Company, 1992), 115.
4. 2 Corinthians 1:9-10 (World English Bible).

John Reekie's photograph of St. Paul's Episcopal Church was originally a stereograph. (The above image is the cropped right plate). This was taken in April 1865 on Grace Street in Richmond, Virginia. Because Richmond was the capital of the Confederacy, General Robert E. Lee as well as President Jefferson Davis worshiped at St. Paul's. Dr. Charles Minnigerode served as the church's priest during the Civil War.[1]

Communion and Re-union

It had been a very eventful Spring. Lee surrendered to Grant at Appomattox Court House. Abraham Lincoln was assassinated at the Ford Theater in Washington D.C. Hostilities had ceased, the rifles had been stacked, and the Rebel soldiers were told to go home and be good citizens.

Not too awfully far from Appomattox Court House, worshippers gathered in Richmond, Virginia at St. Paul's Episcopal Church. It was a Sunday morning in June of 1865. Nearly two months had passed since Lee's surrender. After four years of brutal war, these parishioners may have devoutly hoped to find respite from conflict that morning.

The priest prepared to offer the Lord's Supper. Immediately after the invitation was issued, a tall, well-dressed former slave descended from the balcony and was the first to kneel at the altar.

The white members of the congregation were frozen in their pews at what they considered a breach of order. Negroes weren't to come to the table with white folks! Even the priest was unsure what to do.

In this moment of silent outrage, a distinguished man with a white beard rose from his pew and made his way to the altar rail. He knelt near the black man. The white man was instantly recognizable to the church members—the former general in chief of the armies of the Confederacy, Robert E. Lee himself!

The tension was broken. The remainder of the congregation rose to approach the throne of grace and receive the tokens of Christ's body and blood.

What exactly did Lee mean to convey by his action? This is where history often becomes a matter of interpretation. One eyewitness who reported the events of that morning was a former Confederate officer, whose perspective was no doubt influenced by his own racial attitudes.

Col. T. L. Broun, writing many years after the war, reported his disgust toward the former slave who knelt to receive the Lord's Supper. He describes the church members as:

> ... being deeply chagrined at this attempt to inaugurate the "new regime" to offend and humiliate them during their most devoted Church services.

Broun continues, offering his own view of Lee's response:

> General Robert E. Lee ... ignoring the action and presence of the negro ... reverently knelt down to partake of the communion, and not far from the negro. This lofty conception of duty by Gen. Lee under such provoking and irritating circumstances had a magic effect upon the other communicants (including the writer), who went forward to the communion table. By this action of Gen. Lee the services were conducted as if the negro had not been present.[2]

But I think the truth is more complicated. Robert E. Lee himself declared that in his eyes the Civil War had never been about slavery, but rather about state sovereignty vs. federal sovereignty. In an interview with Lee just weeks after his surrender at Appomattox Court House, Thomas M. Cook reported Lee's view of slavery. He quotes Lee as saying:

> The best men of the South have long been anxious to do away with this institution, and were quite willing today to see it abolished. They consider slavery forever dead.[3]

Years later, Lee reiterated these views to the Reverend Dr. John Leyburn: *I am rejoiced that slavery is abolished.*[4]

I believe that Lee's intention that morning was likely very different than Broun's interpretation. By kneeling at the altar rail with a former slave, he made it clear that, "There is neither Jew nor Greek, there is neither slave nor free man, there is neither male nor female; for you are all one in Christ Jesus."[5]

Our Lord, you have broken down the walls of separation between people, and you are our Peace. May we find opportunities for reconciliation within families, churches, and within our nation. Amen.

Notes

1. *Richmond, Virginia. St. Paul's Episcopal church. (Grace Street)* (Library of Congress, cwp2003005712/PP).
2. "Negro Communed at St. Paul's Church" *Confederate Veteran* 13 (August, 1905):360. It is presumed that Colonel Broun wrote this article himself a few months after he told this story during an interview which appeared in the April 16, 1905 issue of the *Richmond Times-Dispatch*.
3. Thomas M. Cook, "Mr. Thomas M. Cook's Despatch, Richmond, Va., April 24, 1865: General Robert E. Lee" *New York Herald*, April 29, 1865, 5.
4. John Leyburn, "An Interview with General Robert E. Lee" *Century Illustrated Monthly Magazine* 30 (May, 1885): 166-167.
5. Galatians 3:28 (World English Bible).

Nathan Bedford Forrest was one of the most effective and ruthless Confederate cavalry generals in the Civil War. Today he is also one of the most controversial figures of the Civil War and Reconstruction, even after more than 150 years.[1]

Forrest's Repentance

He has been called a tactical military genius. He has been called a war criminal. His name has been associated with the rise of the Ku Klux Klan. He has been praised *and* criticized for defending the rights of freed slaves to vote. He was one of the most controversial figures of the Confederacy during and after the Civil War—General Nathan Bedford Forrest.

Before his home state of Tennessee seceded from the Union, Forrest had amassed a huge fortune from the slave trade and from cotton plantations worked by armies of slaves.

During the Civil War, his leadership was regarded as the decisive difference in several battles. It was said of him that *he was the only Confederate cavalryman of whom Grant stood in much dread.*[2] His military philosophy as a cavalry commander has become a standard for mobilized warfare today—*Get there first with the most men.*[3]

He was famous for his personal courage, military genius, and daring. He was known to singlehandedly fight off multiple Union soldiers simultaneously in hand-to-hand combat.

But there were also stains on his reputation. He was in command of the Confederate cavalry brigade that allegedly massacred hundreds of

Negro soldiers and their families at Fort Pillow on April 12, 1864. Although historians debate the details of this incident, it still casts a shadow over Forrest's war record.

And after the Civil War was over, Forrest was a prominent member of the Ku Klux Klan.[4] Former Confederate soldiers had founded the KKK as a means of resistance to the Federal Reconstruction of the South. They physically intimidated former slaves, especially those who now participated in the political processes of election. Their tactics grew increasingly violent. No wonder, then, that in our modern retrospective, we look back on Nathan Bedford Forrest with a critical eye.

However, what we may miss is the rest of the story. By 1868, Forrest had renounced his ties to the KKK. He had even been invited in July 1875 to speak to an organization of Black southerners in Memphis, Tennessee. In his speech, he said this:

> I want to elevate you to take positions in law offices, in stores, on farms, and wherever you are capable of going ... You have a right to elect whom you please; vote for the man you think best, and I think, when that is done, that you and I are freemen ... Go to work, be industrious, live honestly and act truly, and when you are oppressed I'll come to your relief. I thank you, ladies and gentlemen, for this opportunity you have afforded me to be with you, and to assure you that I am with you in heart and in hand.[5]

Obviously, this former slave-owner, ruthless warrior, and member of a racist hate-group had come a long way. There is one clear cause of this change— Forrest was experiencing "spiritual conviction." Through the Christian witness of a former military comrade, the preaching of the Gospel, and the persistent prayers of a Christian wife, Forrest was experiencing the early stages of conversion.

On the evening of November 14, 1875, Nathan Forrest was sitting with his wife Mary Ann at the Court Street Cumberland Presbyterian Church in Memphis. Rev. Stainback preached on the wise and foolish builders from Matthew 7:24-27. The pastor's words, about the consequences of building one's life on sand, struck Forrest to the heart. He took Rev. Stainback aside after the service. The minister later described Forrest's reaction:

I saw he was silent and seemed somewhat agitated. I did not suspicion the cause. Presently he stopped abruptly, and fixing his piercing gaze upon me, said: "Sir, your sermon tonight has removed the last prop from me. I am the fool who has built his house upon the sand; I am a miserable, lost sinner."

The very next day, Forrest met with the pastor again. They read the Bible and prayed together, and Forrest placed his trust in Christ for salvation.[6]

Nathan Bedford Forrest's conversion confirms the claims of the Gospel of Jesus Christ, that: "if anyone is in Christ, he is a new creation. The old things have passed away. Behold, all things have become new."[7]

Even a "man of blood" and former slave owner like Nathan Bedford Forrest can be redeemed.

Our Lord, thank you for amazing grace that not only pardons us, but also cleanses us of all sin, and transforms us into the people you mean for us to be. Amen.

Notes

1. *General Nathan B. Forrest* (Lib. of Congress, brh2009000003/PP)
2. Shelby Foote, *The Civil War: A Narrative* (New York: Random, 1963) 3 vols., 2: 65.
3. Basil Wilson Duke, *Reminiscences of General Basil W. Duke* (New York: Doubleday, Page & Company, 1911), 346.
4. As with so many aspects of Forrest's life, his role in the Klan is also controversial. Some sources allege that he was elected the "Grand Wizard" while others dispute that.
5. Forrest was invited to speak to the Independent Order of Pole-Bearers Association. *Memphis Daily Appeal*, July 6, 1875, 1.
6. Rev. Stainback recounted this event in his funeral message, which was printed in the *Memphis Daily Appeal*, November 1, 1877, 4.
7. 2 Corinthians 5:17 (World English Bible).

This photograph of the Capitol Dome was taken on March 4, 1861 at Abraham Lincoln's first inauguration. There is no majestic dome capping this great symbol of American democracy. In 1861, when this monumental dome was unfinished, the American democracy was also unfinished. The nation that was founded on the proclamation of liberty and equality was still a contradiction. The project of American democracy was unfinished then. American democracy is unfinished still.[1]

What Does It Mean?

The day we visited Gettysburg was dramatic for me. It was near the end of the day. There was virtually no one in sight. Ominous storm clouds loomed on the horizon. Thunder rumbled in the distance.

I clambered alone to the crest of the Little Round Top. As I looked out over the battlefield, I heard the boom of thunder. This is what the report of cannons must have sounded like on July 3, 1863.

Suddenly it was all very real.

When I got back to the car, my wife turned to me and said, "Why do you want to be in a place where all these men died?" She had also deeply felt the reality of that battle so long ago. She saw Gettysburg as a place of horror and death.

I have asked myself her question many times over the years. Why am I so interested in this violent, divisive era? Why do I keep returning to Civil War battlefields?

The answers are complex. As a young boy, I was drawn to the raw courage of the soldiers on both sides. I could see the obvious justice of the Union side—fighting against slavery—so my bias ran in favor of the soldiers clothed in blue.

Since then, I've spent most of my adult life in the South, and I'm much more aware of historical ambiguities. I am still sure of the injustice of slavery. But I also know that the war wasn't only about slavery.

On January 2, 1864, Confederate General Patrick Cleburne proposed that slavery be abolished. He truly believed that the war was about state sovereignty, not slavery.[2]

Even Abraham Lincoln, although he strongly believed that slavery was immoral, saw that the immediate crisis for the nation was first and foremost about preserving the Union, not abolishing slavery:

> My paramount object in this struggle is to save the Union, and is not either to save or destroy Slavery. If I could save the Union without freeing any slave, I would do it; and if I could save it by freeing all the slaves, I would do it; and if I could do it by freeing some and leaving others alone, I would also do that ... I have here stated my purpose according to my view of official duty, and I intend no modification of my oft-expressed personal wish that all men, everywhere, could be free.[3]

The Civil War still matters. It matters because it was the violent setting for one of the great debates of history. The issues that created that great conflict are like ghosts arising from time to time to haunt us. America's conflict over federal versus state sovereignty is still very much alive. Inequality and racial discrimination still linger like a noxious fog.

Each side strongly believed in the moral superiority of their cause. Abraham Lincoln made reference to this paradox in his Second Inaugural Address: *Both read the same Bible and pray to the same God, and each invoke His aid against the other.*[4]

Despite this paradox, I believe this is where our hope lies today— in the one God to whom we pray and whose Bible we read.

Near the end of the Civil War, Lincoln was interested in reconciling and healing a divided and wounded nation. He concluded his Second Inaugural Address on March 4, 1865 with this exhortation:

> *With malice toward none, with charity for all, with firmness in the right as God gives us to see the right, let us strive on to finish the work we are in, to bind up the nation's wounds, to care for him who shall*

have borne the battle and for his widow and his orphan, to do all
which may achieve and cherish a just and a lasting peace among
ourselves and with all nations.[5]

I believe this is one of the lasting lessons we can take from the bloody Civil War. We still face unresolved conflicts that have endured since those days. But if we are Christians, we are to be agents of reconciliation and healing in our own times, no matter how ambiguous the issues may seem today. We do well to heed the words of St. Paul:

" ... all things are of God, who reconciled us to himself through Jesus
Christ, and gave to us the ministry of reconciliation; namely, that
God was in Christ reconciling the world to himself, not reckoning to
them their trespasses, and having committed to us the word of
reconciliation. We are therefore ambassadors on behalf of Christ, as
though God were entreating by us: we beg you on behalf of Christ,
be reconciled to God."[6]

And this brings me back to my original question—why am I still so fascinated by the Civil War?

The answer is that we are not so different from our divided ancestors. We are still conflicted and divided over many issues. Therefore, as Christians who are reconciled to God through Christ, we must confront the conflicts of our day as ambassadors of reconciliation.

Our Lord, conflicts and differences still divide us today—as Christians, as
Americans, as citizens of the world. You have reconciled us to yourself.
Empower us to be reconcilers rather than dividers, with malice toward
none and charity for all. Amen.

Notes

1. *Inauguration of President Lincoln at U.S. Capitol, March 4, 1861* (Library of Congress, 00650936).
2. Proposal of Patrick R. Cleburne, major-general, January 2, 1864, *The War of the Rebellion: A Compilation of the Official Records of the Union and Confederate Armies*, series 1, vol. 52, part 2, 586-592.
3. "President Lincoln's Letter" *New York Daily Tribune*, Saturday, August 25, 1862, 4.

   Abraham Lincoln wrote this on August 22, 1862, in response to an editorial letter that Horace Greeley published on August 20. "The Prayer of Twenty Millions" was the title of Greely's open letter to the president, dated August 19. Greeley was an abolitionist who used his position as the founder and editor of the New York Tribune to promote his views.
4. Page 3 of Lincoln's inaugural address can be seen at The Abraham Lincoln Papers at the Library of Congress: Series 3. General Correspondence. 1837-1897. *Abraham Lincoln, [March 4, 1865] (Second Inaugural Address; endorsed by Lincoln, April 10, 1865* (Library of Congress).
5. Ibid., 4.
6. 2 Corinthians 5:18-20 (World English Bible).

EPILOGUE

Why Another Book About the Civil War?

I return to the question raised in my *Introduction—Why another book about the Civil War?* And more specifically—why a <u>devotional</u> book about the Civil War?

Accounts of life in camp during the Civil War reveal that soldiers then were pretty much like soldiers of any era—they marched and drilled, they gambled and smoked, they sang and they talked about home.

And they also yearned for spiritual comfort and strength. Religious revival services recorded great response from the soldiers. Bibles were distributed. There was a hunger among many soldiers to know God and his will for themselves and their nation, whether they represented the Union or the Confederacy.

I also believe that the fundamental issues that created the Great Crisis of the Civil War are theological issues. In the language of the Declaration of Independence, the *self-evident truths* are theological matters: *that all men are created equal, that they are endowed by their Creator with certain unalienable rights; that among these rights are life, liberty and the pursuit of happiness.* But not all men and women enjoyed these "unalienable rights."

The Civil War was a conflict that had at its root the question about the very nature of what it means to be a human being. As Abraham Lincoln said eloquently in1858, even before he was elected president:

As I would not be a slave, so I would not be a master. This expresses my idea of democracy. Whatever differs from this, to the extent of the difference, is no democracy.[1] And six years later, during his presidency, he wrote: *If slavery is not wrong, then nothing is wrong.*[2]

In a sense, slavery was the Original Sin of American Democracy. And if slavery was the Original Sin of the American Democracy, the Civil War was an expiation in blood for that sin.

Responsible political historians will point out that the Civil War was also about more than slavery. The nation was attempting to resolve unfinished business about its very identity. Were we a nation of states, each with its own independent sovereignty and autonomy? Or were we a nation that was indivisible and united as a federal republic, with a strong central government? But these are political questions.

My purpose in writing this devotional book was to remind us that God is to be found even in the horrors and the ambiguities of such a time as that. We are all connected to the past, and what we do in the present does have implications for the future. Through it all, God is Lord over time and history. Revelation tells us: "I am the Alpha and the Omega," says the Lord God, "who is and who was and who is to come, the Almighty."[3]

Time and history are ultimately all in God's hands.

Notes

1. Roy P. Basler, editor, "Definition of Democracy" *The Collected Works of Abraham Lincoln. 8 vols.* (New Brunswick: Rutgers University Press, 1953), 2:352.
2. The Abraham Lincoln Papers at the Library of Congress: Series 1. General Correspondence. 1833-1916. *Abraham Lincoln to Albert G. Hodges, Monday, April 07, 1864 (Lincoln's position on slavery)* (Library of Congress).
3. Revelation 1:8 (World English Bible).

INDEX

Index